Russian Pr

St. Peter and St. Paul; the S

Ostrog at Omsk; the story of Siberian exile;

Tiumen, Tomsk, Saghalien

Arthur Griffiths

Alpha Editions

INTRODUCTION

The huge empire founded by the Czars of Russia in the latter half of the sixteenth century was based upon absolute autocracy. The Czar by virtue of his divine origin exercised absolute authority over the many diverse elements consolidated under his sovereign will. From the earliest times no idea of personal liberty was tolerated; the slightest expression of independence in thought and action was peremptorily forbidden. The attitude of the government has ever been uncompromisingly severe toward all malcontents, and Russian history for the last two centuries is one long record of conspiracy constantly afoot, and constantly repressed by savagely cruel coercion. Imprisonment, the absolute loss of physical freedom, has taken a wider meaning in Russia than in other countries, for it is the lot in one form or another of two classes of offenders: the ordinary criminal under a civil code, from which capital punishment is now excluded, and the political dissidents deemed criminal by the arbitrary government of the land and deserving of exemplary and vindictive punishment. Russian prisons are in some respects the worst and most horrible the world has seen, and they are more especially reprehensible in these latter days when humane considerations are allowed weight in the administration of penal institutions.

In giving a description of Russian prisons as they have been and to some extent still remain, it is fair to state that the facts are authenticated by unimpeachable evidence. We have the statements of eye-witnesses speaking from their own knowledge, and these unsparing critics have not always been foreigners and outsiders; Russians themselves have also raised their indignant voices in energetic protest, and official reports can be quoted to substantiate many of the charges. On the other hand, Russian methods have found champions and apologists among travellers, who were, perhaps, superficial observers, easily misled, and their accounts cannot in the least upset the conclusions arrived at by more thoroughgoing and disinterested investigators. Such men as George Kennan, indefatigable, honest, courageous and of the highest veracity, have framed an indictment from which there is no appeal. The facts have been vouched for, moreover, by the trustworthy narratives of those who have themselves been personal victims of the worst horrors inflicted, and buttressed by confidential reports from great Russian functionaries sent direct to the Czar. Secret despatches which have fallen into hands for which they were not intended, and have been made public by the searchers for truth, frankly admit the justice of the sentence passed upon at least one frightful portion of Russian penal institutions,—the system of exile to Eastern Siberia. Governor-General Anuchin twice addressed the Czar Alexander III, in 1880 and 1882, after long tours of personal inspection, in such condemnatory terms that the mighty ruler upon whom the terrible burden of responsibility rested, was moved to endorse the report in his own handwriting with the words, "It is inexcusable, even criminal, to allow such a state of affairs in Siberia to continue." The frightful system which allowed an irresponsible bureaucracy to sentence untried persons to exile by so-called "administrative process" is fully explained and described in the present volume.

CHAPTER I
GENERAL SURVEY

Commencement of judicial reform in Russia—Abandonment of knout and branding iron—The plet—Two classes of prisons, the "lock-up" and the "central" or convict prisons—Experiences of a woman exiled from Russia—Testimony of Carl Joubert—The state of the central prisons—The "model" prison in St. Petersburg—Punishments inflicted—The food in different prisons—Attempted escapes—Myshkin—His early history and daring exploits—Failure of his plan to rescue Chernyshevski from Siberia—His escape, recapture, and sentence of death—The prisoner Medvediev.

A definite movement toward judicial reform began in Russia in the early sixties. The old law courts with their archaic procedure and evil repute as sinks of bribery and corruption were abolished. Trial by jury was revived, and justices of the peace were established to dispose of the smaller criminal offences. Shortly afterward, two of the most disgraceful features in the Russian penal code, the knout and the branding iron, disappeared. The punishment of splitting the nostrils to mark ineffaceably the prisoners exiled to the salt mines of Okhotsk also ceased, and the simple Chinese no longer were surprised with the sight of a hitherto unknown race of men with peculiar features of their own. The knout, however, had long served its devilish purpose. It was inflicted even upon women in the time of Peter the Great, and was still remembered as an instrument which would surely kill at the thirtieth stroke, although in the hands of a skilful performer a single blow might prove fatal.

Flogging did not go entirely out of practice and might still be ordered by peasant courts, in the army and in the convict prisons. But another brutal whip survived; the plet is still used in the far-off penal settlements, although rarely, and only upon the most hardened offenders. It is composed of a thong of twisted hide about two feet in length, ending in a number of thin lashes, each a foot long, with small leaden balls attached, and forms a most severe and murderous weapon. The number of strokes inflicted may vary from twenty-three to fifty and at Saghalien in some cases reaches ninety-nine. If the victim has money or friends, the flogger is bribed to lay on heavily; for when the blow is so light as to fail to draw blood, the pain is greater. By beginning gently the flagellator can gradually increase the force of each blow until the whole back is covered with long swollen transverse welts which not uncommonly mortify, causing death.

At one time trial by court-martial could sentence a soldier to the frightful ordeal of the "rods," flogging administered by comrades standing in two ranks between which he moved at a deliberate pace while they "laid on" the strokes with sticks upon his bare back. This is exactly the same penalty as that of "running the gauntlet," or "gantlope," well known in old-time military practice, and sometimes called "Green Street" in Russia, for the rods used were not always stripped of their leaves. The infliction might be greatly prolonged and the number of strokes given sometimes amounted to several thousand. Devilish ingenuity has now replaced the physical torture of knout and plet by a modern device for inflicting bodily discomfort, nothing less than riveting a wheelbarrow to a man's legs, which he must take with him everywhere, even to bed,—the apology for a bed on which he passed the night.

Russian prisons are of several classes. There are first the "lock-ups," or places of detention for the accused awaiting trial, scattered throughout the country, and quite unequal in the aggregate to the accommodation of the number of prisoners on hand. It has been estimated that to lodge all adequately, half as many more than the existing prisons would be required. Those of another class, the houses of correction, the hard labour or "central" prisons where compulsory labour is exacted, are very much like the "public works" convict prisons in the English system. Many of these are established in European Russia; more are to be found in Western Siberia, and, on somewhat different lines, in the penal settlements of Eastern Siberia.

In the provincial "lock-ups" or *ostrogs* the conditions have always been deplorable. They are horribly overcrowded with wretched, hopeless beings for whom trial is often greatly delayed, and who lie there in inconceivable discomfort at the mercy of brutal and extortionate gaolers, "packed like herrings in a cask, in rooms of inconceivable foulness, in an atmosphere that sickens even to insensibility any one entering from the open air," says one writer.

The same author gives the experiences of a lady who was expelled from Russia for opening a school for peasants' children, and who was transferred to the Prussian frontier from prison to prison. "At Wilna," she says, "we were taken to the town prison, and detained for two hours late at night in an open yard under a drenching rain. At last we were pushed into a dark corridor and counted. Two soldiers laid hold of me and insulted me shamefully. After many oaths and much foul language, the fire was lighted and I found myself in a spacious room, in which it was impossible to take a step in any direction without treading on the women sleeping on the floor. Two women who occupied a bed took pity on me and invited me to share it with them.... The next night we were turned out from the prison and paraded in the yard for the start under a heavy rain. I do not know how I happened to escape the fists of the gaolers, as the prisoners did not understand the evolutions and performed them under a storm of blows and curses; those who protested were put in irons and sent so to the train, although the law prescribes that in the cellular wagons no prisoner shall be chained.

"Arrived at Kovno, we spent the whole day in going from one police station to another. In the evening we were taken to the prison for women where the superintendent was railing against the head gaoler and swearing that she would give him 'bloody teeth.' The prisoners told me that she often kept promises of this sort. Here I spent a week among murderesses and thieves and women arrested by mistake. Misfortune unites the unfortunate, and everybody tried to make life more tolerable for the rest; all were very kind to me and did their best to console me. On the previous day I had eaten nothing, for prisoners receive no food on the day they are brought to prison. I fainted from hunger, and the prisoners brought me round by giving me some of their black bread; there was a female inspector, but she did nothing but shout out shameless oaths such as no drunken man would use.

"After a week's halt at Kovno, I was sent on to the next town. After three days' march we came to Mariampol. My feet were wounded and my stockings full of blood. The soldiers advised me to ask for a vehicle, but I preferred physical suffering to the continued cursing and foul language of the chiefs. I was taken before the commander, who remarked that as I had walked for three days I could very well manage a fourth. On arrival at Volkovisk, the last halt, we were lodged provisionally in the prison, but the female side was in ruins and we were taken to the men's quarters, and had nowhere to sit but on the filthily dirty and foul-smelling floor. Here I spent two days and nights, passing the whole time at the window. In the night, the door was constantly thrown open for new arrivals; they also brought in a male lunatic who was perfectly naked. The miserable prisoners delighted in this, and tormented the maniac into a paroxysm of passion, until at last he fell on the floor in a fit and lay there foaming at the mouth. On the third day a soldier of the depot, a Jew, took me into his room, a tiny cell, where I stayed with his wife.

"The prisoners told me that many of them were detained by mistake for seven or eight months, awaiting their papers before being sent across the frontier. It is easy to imagine their condition after a seven months' stay in this sewer without a change of linen.... I had been six weeks on the road and was still delayed, but I got leave to send a registered letter to St. Petersburg, where I had influential friends, and a telegram came to send me on to Prussia immediately. My papers were soon found, and I was sent to Eydtkuhnen, where I was set at liberty."

It is asserted by our author that this horrible picture was not one whit overcharged. "To Russians every word rings true and every scene looks normal. Oaths, filth, brutality, bribery, blows, hunger, are the essentials of every *ostrog* and of every depot from Kovno to Kamtchatka, from Archangel to Erzerum." It is summed up by Kropotkin as follows: "The incredible duration of preliminary detention, the disgusting circumstances of daily life; the congregation of hundreds of prisoners into small dirty chambers; the flagrant immorality of a corps of jailers who are practically omnipotent, whose whole function is to terrorise and oppress; the want of labour and the total absence of all that contributes to the moral welfare of man; the cynical contempt for human dignity and the physical degradation of prisoners— these are the elements of prison life in Russia."

Another writer of more recent date, Carl Joubert, whose works on Russia have been widely read, says, "I am aware that in no part of the world is the lot of a prisoner a happy one. It is not intended that it should be; but in civilised countries they are, at least, given the opportunity of keeping themselves clean and decent. They are treated as human beings and their health is considered; but in Russia it is different. The prisoners in Russia, whether before or after the trial—and a great many of the political prisoners have no trial—the Russian prisoners are considered beasts, and treated accordingly. The warders know what is expected of them; and if a warder shows any glimmering of humanity in his treatment of the prisoners committed to his charge, his services are dispensed with and a stronger-hearted warder takes his place.

"I said that Russian prisoners have no sex; but I must qualify that statement. In so far as the normal treatment of the women is concerned, they are separated from the men, but no other distinction is made. If they are young and attractive, however, their sex can procure for them, and worse still, for those who are dear to them, a certain amount of consideration from those in authority over them on the road to Siberia."

The penalties inflicted by the Russian code may be classed under four heads. The first is hard labour with the loss of civil rights, so that the convict's property passes to his heirs; he is dead in law, and his wife may marry another; he endures his term either after deportation to Siberia, or in one of the "central prisons" which have been built on purpose in European Russia, and where he spends a third or fourth of his entire sentence, until he goes finally to Siberia or Saghalien as a penal colonist. These central prisons were created to substitute a more regular and more severe treatment than was possible at a distance from home, and the aim was achieved. According to the best authorities, the central prisons are practically "hells upon earth." "The horrors of hard labour in Siberia," says Peter Kropotkin, "have paled before them, and all those who have had experience of them are unanimous in declaring that the day a prisoner starts for Siberia is the happiest in his life."

A few specific details may be quoted about one or two of these prisons. In that of Kharkov, in Little Russia, at one time two hundred of the five entered, and the fugitive was caught in a trap. He was transferred to another cell from which there was no prospect of escape.

Myshkin, hopeless and reckless, now sought freedom in death. Resolving to commit an offence which would entail capital punishment, he obtained leave to attend divine service at the prison church, and managed to get close to the governor, whom he struck in the face when in the act of kissing the cross in the hands of the officiating priest. Under ordinary conditions, trial and condemnation to death would follow, but just at this time the distressing state of affairs at Kharkov had caused so much uneasiness that the Minister of the Interior had sent a sanitary expert to report upon the conditions which had produced so much lunacy and so many deaths. Professor Dobroslavin pronounced the place unfit for human habitation, and urged the immediate removal of all political convicts. It was no doubt supposed that Myshkin was of unsound mind when he struck the governor, and he was not even tried for the offence, but shortly afterward was despatched to the far-off silver mines of Kara.

Myshkin's antecedents and his ultimate fate are of interest. He was a young student at the Technological Institute of St. Petersburg in 1870, when, fired by the ardent spirit of the new revolutionists, he conceived a bold project to effect the escape of the well-known author and political writer, Chernyshevski, at that time in Siberian exile. After spending some time in the old Alexandrovski central prison near Irkutsk, the prisoner was presently interned under police surveillance in Villuisk, a small village in the subarctic province of Yakutsk. Myshkin planned to travel across Asia disguised as a captain of gendarmerie, present a forged order to the head of the police at Villuisk, desiring him to hand over Chernyshevski to the sham captain, who was to escort him to another place on the Amur river. Myshkin got safely to Irkutsk, where he was employed in the office of the gendarmerie and became greatly trusted. He had the freedom of the office and cleverly abstracted the necessary blank forms, forged the signatures, affixed the seals, got his uniform, and, thus provided with all proper credentials, appeared before the *ispravnik*, or local chief of police, at Villuisk, who received him with all deference and respect. Myshkin was a man of fine presence, eloquent and well spoken, and when he produced his order he was within an ace of success.

But there was a weak point in the plot. It was quite unusual for officers of rank to travel without escort, and Myshkin had not had sufficient funds to take with him confederates disguised as soldiers or gensdarmes. The *ispravnik* grew suspicious, the more so as the exile Chernyshevski was an important political offender, and he hesitated to surrender him without seeing his way more clearly. He told Myshkin that he must have the authority of the governor to set his exile free. Myshkin, unabashed, offered to go in person to seek the governor's consent, and he set off for Yakutsk, attended by a complimentary escort of Cossacks. The *ispravnik* astutely sent another Cossack to pass them on the road with a letter of advice for the governor. The messenger caught up with the first party and made no secret of his mission.

The game was up, and Myshkin, in despair, made a bolt for the woods. The Cossacks promptly gave chase, but Myshkin drew his revolver, beat off his pursuers and succeeded in getting away. He wandered through the forests for a week, and was at last captured, half dead from cold and privation. He was lodged first in the prison of Irkutsk and then brought to St. Petersburg, where he was thrown into the fortress of St. Peter and St. Paul, and he lay there for three years in a solitary cell awaiting trial. He was kept in the Trubetzkoi Bastion, near a prisoner whom Mr. Kennan afterward met in Siberia and who described his neighbour's sufferings feelingly. "Myshkin," he said, "was often delirious from fever, excitement or the maddening effect of long solitary confinement, and I frequently heard his cries when he was put into a strait-jacket or strapped to his bed by the fortress guard."

Myshkin's trial caused a great sensation. The government had refused to allow the proceedings to be taken down in shorthand, and the prisoner declined to make any defence; he made a fiery speech, however, denouncing the secrecy of the trial and declaring that the public ought to hear the whole case through the press. He was ordered out of court, and being removed by force, his last words, half stifled, were: "This court is worse than a house of ill-fame; there they sell only bodies, but here you prostitute honour, justice and law." This insult aggravated the original offence, and the court increased his sentence to ten years' penal servitude with forfeiture of all civil rights.

Myshkin was a born orator, but by his own admission he lived to regret his eloquence. When on his long journey to Eastern Siberia, one of his comrades died at Irkutsk, and he was moved to make a brief oration at the funeral. He spoke out in church, eulogising the high moral character of the deceased, and declaring that "out of the ashes of this heroic man and others like him will grow the tree of liberty for Russia." Here the police interfered; Myshkin was dragged out of church and sentenced later to an additional fifteen years' penal servitude. So it was said of him that he never made but two speeches in his life, one of which cost him ten and the other fifteen years of imprisonment. Myshkin regretted the second speech, which, he said, would do no good, as the world could not hear; it was the mere gratification of a personal impulse, and it added so many years to his detention, that, even if he lived to emerge from exile, he would be too aged to work effectively in the cause of Russian freedom.

Myshkin afterward escaped from Kara, when a more rigorous régime had been introduced by Count Loris Melikov, and permission to work in the had died, the majority of them carried off by consumption. Twenty out of forty-eight was a large proportion, and the fact is authenticated by M. Petit, who can give the names and exact dates.

After the year 1896, the rigours of the régime were in some measure slackened. Books were allowed, such as scientific manuals, grammars and dictionaries for the study of languages, and historical books of a date previous to the eighteenth century, but no works of a purely literary character and no periodicals, reviews or newspapers. Writing materials were issued, a few sheets during the daytime, which, with whatever was written thereon, were withdrawn in the evening. By degrees the dietary was slightly improved, the period of exercise was prolonged and the prisoners were occasionally allowed to work in the garden or in the carpenter's shop. Still better, association with a fellow prisoner for a brief space was conceded twice a week when at exercise. Later, extracts from the letters of relatives were read out to the prisoner once yearly, communicating a brief message such as, "We are alive and well and living at such and such a place." By and by the prisoners were permitted to reply no less briefly, but never to state where they were confined.

Two provincial prisons were much concerned with political prisoners, those of Kiev and Moscow. The former was the scene of many tragic episodes, and fierce conflicts between the revolutionists and the authorities. Some remarkable escapes were made from them. The university of Kiev was a hot-bed of political unrest, and its students were active and determined conspirators. An independent spirit was always present in the prison, the product of past resistance. It was from Kiev that the well-known Leo Deutsch escaped with two others in 1878, through the courageous assistance of a comrade Frolenko, who managed as a free man to get a false passport and obtain employment as a warder in the prison. He took the name of Michael and was in due course appointed to take charge of the corridor in which his friends Deutsch, Stefanovich and Bohanovsky were located. They had pretended to protest against his coming to their ward so as to disarm suspicion.

Frolenko set to work without loss of time. He provided disguises, two suits of private clothes and a warder's uniform, which the prisoners put on, and he then released them from their cells. As they were stumbling along the passage, one of them tripped against a rope which he caught at and pulled frantically. It proved to be the alarm bell of the prison and caused a deafening noise. The false "Michael" at once explained to the authorities what he had done unwittingly, and the disturbance passed off without further discovery. Again the fugitives, who had hidden themselves in the first corners they found, started on their journey and got out of the prison, where a confederate met the party and led them to the river and to a boat stored with provisions which awaited them. They voyaged along the Dnieper for a whole week, concealing themselves when necessary in the long rushes, and at last reached Krementchug, where they were furnished with passports and money and successfully passed the frontier. "Michael" went with them, and it was long supposed by the officials that he had been made away with by the prison breakers.

Beverley, a young man of English extraction, met death when escaping from the Kiev prison. He had been arrested for living under a false passport and being active in the revolutionary propaganda with a comrade Isbitski. He had driven a tunnel from their cell to a point beyond the prison walls. The authorities had discovered the tunnel and had posted a party of soldiers at the exit, where the fugitives must emerge into the upper air. As soon as they appeared they were shot down. Beverley was mortally wounded, and as he lay on the ground he was despatched by repeated bayonet stabs. Isbitski was also struck down, but was carried back alive after a severe beating.

Leo Deutsch gives other cases of escape that proved more successful. A student Ivanov was helped to freedom by the officer commanding the guard, Tihonov, who was a member of the *Narodnaya Volya* society, or the "Will of the People." Another prisoner disappeared under the most mysterious circumstances which were never explained. But the most important escape was in August, 1902, when eleven noted prisoners, arrested a short time before, broke prison in a body. They exercised every evening in the prison yard which was bounded on one side by an outer wall overlooking fields and which was unguarded on the outside. The prisoners got into the field, taking with them an iron anchor weighing twenty pounds, and a rope ladder. At a given moment some of them had fallen upon their warder, overpowered him, gagged and bound him. Two others, climbing on each other's shoulders, reached the top of the wall, where they pulled up the anchor, made it fast, and then secured the rope ladder, which served for the ascent of the prisoners on one side and their descent on the other. So much sympathy was felt for them in the town that they were effectually concealed when at large and provided with the necessary funds for leaving the country. Throughout the whole affair no blood was shed and no one was hurt. Many more escaped from Kiev in a different fashion, passing out of its walls to the scaffold.

The great central prison of Moscow, locally known as the "Butirki," served as a general depot for ordinary criminals on the point of departure as exiles about to be transported to Siberia. It is a vast establishment with accommodation for thousands; a mighty stone building which looks like a gigantic well. A great wall with a tower at each of the four corners encloses it, and the various classes of politicals were confined in these towers. In the north tower were the "administrative" exiles; in the "chapel" tower were those still under examination, and in another the female prisoners were kept.

entreaties of human beings who were being subjected to torture, but whose sufferings were not acute enough to seek expression in shrieks or high pitched cries.... No attempt was made by the singers to pitch their voices in harmony or pronounce the words in unison. There were no pauses or rests at the ends of the lines, no distinctly marked rhythm. The singers seemed to be constantly breaking in upon one another with slightly modulated variation of the same slow, melancholy air, and the effect produced was that of a rude fugue of a funeral chant." The following is an extract from the words sung:—

"Have pity on us, O our fathers!

Do not forget the unwilling travellers,

Do not forget the long imprisoned.

Feed us, O our fathers—help us!

Feed and help the poor and needy!

Have compassion, O our fathers,

Have compassion, O our mothers,

For the sake of Christ, have mercy

On the prisoners."

"If you can imagine these words, half sung, half chanted slowly, in broken time and in a low key, by hundreds of voices, to an accompaniment made by the jingling and clashing of chains, you will have a faint idea of the song. Rude, artless and inharmonious as the appeal for pity was, I never in my life heard anything so mournful and depressing. It seemed to be the half articulate expression of all the griefs, the misery and the despair that had been felt by generations of human beings in the *étapes*, the forwarding prisons and the mines."

The collections made both in cash and kind were taken on to the next halting place, when they were divided with scrupulous exactitude under the watchful control of the *artel*, or prisoners' association, which rules in every prison with an iron hand.

An advantage enjoyed by the political prisoners in Russian prisons is the affable demeanour of the official staff towards them. Every prison official as a rule treats them with a certain amount of courtesy and respect. This is due to an unwritten law arising from the long established belief that these "politicals" belonged to the educated and cultured classes, and that their offences, so-called, have been committed with high motives, in obedience to the dictates of reason and conscience, in the hope of improving the condition of the people and winning a greater measure of liberty and independence for their down-trodden nation. Superior officers were, as a rule, polite in their address, and subordinates spoke civilly and treated them with marked consideration. The prisoners watched jealously the attitude of their masters toward them, and fiercely resented any failure of respect, or anything that tended to lower their personal dignity.

Leo Deutsch tells a story of the sharp lesson in manners taught to a great functionary, the chief personage and head of the prison department, M. Galkin Vrasski. The incident occurred at Moscow when he was making a tour of inspection through the provincial prisons. The politicals had heard that, conscious of his power and self-importance, he was in the habit of entering cells, when visiting them, with his hat on. The first he reached was occupied by one Dashkievich, who had been a theological student,—"a man of very calm but unyielding temperament, and permeated to an uncommon degree with the instinct of justice and fairness." The great chief entered with much ceremony, escorted by the governor and a brilliant staff, and asked Dashkievich pompously whether he had any complaint to make. "Pardon me," interrupted the prisoner quietly, "it is very impolite of you, sir, to enter my apartment without removing your hat." Vrasski reddened to the roots of his hair, turned on his heel and walked out, followed by his entire entourage.

He was at pains to ask the name of the man who had dared to reprove him thus openly. He had learned his lesson, for he appeared at all the other cells hat in hand. But the offence rankled, and as Deutsch avers, he took his revenge later. Dashkievich had been sentenced to "banishment to the less distant provinces of Siberia;" this was altered by Vrasski's order, and he was sent eventually to Tunka in the furthest wilds, on the border of Mongolia.

In this matter of removing the head-dress, the politicals were very punctilious. Once, on arrival at the Krasnoyarsk prison, which was chiefly cellular, a party of politicals had a serious conflict of opinion with the governor, who ordered that they should be placed in separate cells singly, instead of in association. They resented and positively refused to abide by this order, and demanded to be lodged as heretofore along the road, in company with one another. Pending a change of decision, they remained in the corridor with their baggage, and would not budge a step. The governor of the prison insisted upon compliance with the regulations, and he was backed up by the chief of police, a very blustering and overbearing person. The prisoners would not yield and the matter was referred to higher authority, first to the colonel of gendarmerie, then to the public prosecutor, and lastly to the governor of the district. Nothing could be decided that night, and the prisoners, still obdurate, camped out in the passage, being permitted to have their own way until the district governor had been heard from.

debilitated men, weak women and helpless children, tramping on and on for a whole year or more, shoeless, insufficiently clad and subsisting on the chance alms of the charitable; fed by a meagre pittance, lodged nightly in half-ruinous log prisons, or festering for weeks in detestable forwarding prisons. The Russian exile system has rivalled in its inflictions the cruelties and barbarities of the darkest ages.

By degrees changes in the penal code, multiplying offences punishable by exile, increased the numbers sent to Siberia. The colonisation and development of the new country claimed the attention of the government. Throughout the seventeenth and eighteenth centuries increasing numbers were deported, but with no attempt at organised system and with the most callous neglect of the human beings driven forth like cattle along the dreary road. They were at all times abominably misused everywhere, harassed, whipped, starved, and treated worse than the four-footed beasts, which from their intrinsic value would have been worth a certain amount of care. Exile was substituted for the death penalty, and the families of the offender often accompanied him. The punishment was sometimes accorded for breaking laws and regulations that were most trivial and ridiculous. Among offences were included fortune-telling, prize-fighting, snuff-taking, and driving with reins—a culpable western innovation—for the Russian rode his draught horse then or ran beside it.

The demand for enforced labour steadily increased as Siberia's natural resources became more and more evident. The discovery of mineral wealth, the rich silver mines of Nertchinsk in the Trans-Baikal, and the establishment of large manufactories at Irkutsk called for more exiles, and laws were passed extending the punishment. Any kind of misconduct led to deportation. Jews were exiled for failing to pay their taxes, serfs for cutting down trees without permission, and minor military offences were visited with this penalty. Large numbers took the road, but without the slightest organisation. There was no system; the exiles were driven in troops like cattle from town to town. No one knew exactly the cause of exile or could differentiate between individuals. Some were murderers and the most hardened offenders; some were simple peasants guilty of losing their passports or the victims of an oppressive proprietor. "The exile system," says Kennan, "was nothing but a chaos of disorder in which accident and caprice played almost equally important parts."

Two cases may be quoted here of the haphazard arbitrary treatment that commonly prevailed. A peasant who had innocently bought a stolen horse was sent to Siberia as an enforced colonist, but was not set at liberty on arrival. Through some error and confusion as to his identity, he was transported to the Berozev mines and worked there underground for three and twenty years. Again, the governor of Siberia, Traskin, of notoriously evil repute, having a spite against one of the councillors of the State Chamber, banished him from the province of Irkutsk, with an order that he should never be permitted to remain more than ten days in the same place. The wretched man accordingly spent the rest of his life in aimless wanderings through Siberia.

With the nineteenth century some reforms were introduced. The exiles were organised in parties, marched under escorts, and *étapes*, or halting stations for a stay of a night or more, were built at regular intervals along the road. The identification and separate personality of individuals were established by means of proper papers showing whom they were, their history and destination. A great administrative measure was the creation in 1823 of a central bureau at Tobolsk (removed later to Tiumen) for the record and registration of all exiles arriving and passing into Siberia. Sub-offices at the principal Siberian towns assisted with the necessary details showing the distribution and disposal of all persons banished. Full statistics are consequently available for estimating accurately the extent of penal deportation in recent years. Approximately, since the beginning of the nineteenth century, more than a million souls have passed the boundary line between Europe and Asia. Speaking more exactly, the total number banished between 1823 and 1887 amounted to 772,979, or an annual average of about seventeen thousand.

Siberian exiles have been grouped by Kennan into four great classes. These are as follows: the hard-labour convicts, in Russian called the *katorzhniki*; the penal colonists, or *poselentzy*; the persons merely banished, the *ssylny*; women and children who go to Siberia voluntarily as the companions of fathers and parents, and conversely, in rare cases, men who accompany their wives. Members of this class are called *dobrovolny*. According to law, they are not under the disciplinary control of the escort, but, as a matter of fact, they are subjected to the same treatment as the convicts. An eye-witness reported in a Moscow paper in 1881 that when he met a party of exiles on the march, "the exhausted women and children literally stuck in the mud, and the soldiers dealt them blows to make them advance and keep pace with the rest."

Members of the two first classes wore chains, leg fetters, and walked in slippers for distances of six and seven thousand miles. The rest went free of such physical encumbrances, but were otherwise exposed to the terrible hardships and privations of the long protracted, wearisome march. The mere atmospheric conditions and extremes of temperature in the varying seasons suffice to break down the health of all but the most hardy, for winter succeeded summer before the march ended and vice versa, so that arctic cold alternated with tropical heat, and deep snow with burning sun and torrential rains. When to such exposure are superadded unsuitable clothing, bad and insufficient food, the insanitary condition of the over-crowded *étapes* and the absence of medical care, "one is," Kennan says, "surprised, not that so many die, but that so many get through alive."

A Russian painter, M. Jacoby, has painted an awful picture depicting the frightful scene. It has been graphically described by Kropotkin and may be quoted here in full to give a clear idea of this hideous march.

"You see a marshy plain where the icy wind blows freely, driving before it the snow that begins to cover the frozen soil. Morasses with small shrubs or crumpled trees, bent down by wind or snow, spread as far as the eye can reach; the next village is twenty miles distant. Low mountains, covered with thick pine forests, mingling with the gray snow clouds, rise in the dust on the horizon. A track marked all along by poles to distinguish it from the surrounding plain, ploughed by the passage of thousands of carts, covered with ruts that keep down the hardest wheels, runs through the naked plains. The party slowly moves along this road. In front a row of soldiers opens the march. Behind them heavily advance the hard-labour convicts, with half-shaved heads, wearing gray clothes with a yellow diamond on the back, and open shoes worn out by the long journey, and exhibiting the tatters in which the wounded feet are wrapped. Each convict wears a chain riveted to his ankles, its rings being twisted with rags. The chain goes up each leg and is suspended to a girdle. Another chain closely ties both hands and a third chain binds together six or eight convicts. Every false movement of any of the gang is felt by all his chain companions; the feebler is dragged forward by the stronger and he must not stop the way; the *étape* stage is long and the autumn day is short.

"Behind the hard-labour convicts march the *poselentzy*, condemned to be settled in Siberia, wearing the same gray clothes and the same kind of shoes.... In the rear you discover a few carts drawn by the small, attenuated, cat-like peasants' horses. They are loaded with the bags of the convicts, and with the sick or dying who are fastened by ropes on the top of the load. Behind the carts struggle the wives and children of the convicts; a few have found a free corner on a loaded cart, and crouch there when unable to move further, whilst the great number march behind the carts, leading their children by the hand or bearing them in their arms. In the rear comes a second detachment of soldiers, stimulating these weak, feeble creatures to fresh exertions by blows with the butt end of their muskets."

The infant mortality under these conditions almost exceeds belief, and deportation to Siberia has been aptly and truthfully described as a "massacre of the innocents." In the year 1881, when 2,561 children followed the exile march, very few survived. The majority succumbed to the hardships of the road and died before or immediately after their arrival at their destination.

The yearly quota has constantly increased, numbering from five to eight thousand. To the danger to health incurred must be added the moral degradation, especially in the case of the young girls.

Before reviewing the conditions and setting forth the actual facts, with the processes that produced them, it will be well to dissect the grand totals and arrive at the relative proportions of the three principal classes composing the whole body of exiles constantly moving across the frontier to fill the prisons and to people Siberia to its uttermost ends. Less than one-half were criminal in the sense that they had committed offences and had been adjudged guilty in open court by duly constituted tribunals. The larger moiety had had no legal trial; they had been punished with banishment by the irresponsible action and simple fiat of minor officials and bodies of ill-educated peasants, wielding the extraordinary powers conferred by "administrative process." At no time and in no civilised land have people been so ruthlessly sacrificed and subjected to the forfeiture of personal liberty by this utter abnegation of justice and fair play, and the result is a standing disgrace to the government that permitted and encouraged it. The extent to which this most reprehensible system has obtained may be judged by a simple statement of figures. For many years past the average number sentenced to exile by legal verdict in regular courts was 45.6 per cent. of the whole yearly contingent, and those banished by "administrative process" was 54.4 per cent. It must always be borne in mind that, in describing the methods pursued and the painful results attendant on them, more than half the sufferers were either entirely innocent or guilty of offences that could only be deemed criminal by a strained interpretation of the exercise of authority, and in no case had they been properly tried and convicted by law.

The system has been defined by Mr. Kennan as "the banishment of an obnoxious person from one part of the empire to another without the observance of any of the legal formalities which in most civilised countries precede the deprivation of rights and the restriction of personal liberty." A person might be entirely guiltless of any offence, he need not have made himself amenable to the law; it was enough that the local authorities should suspect him of being "untrustworthy"[1] or believe that his presence in any place was "prejudicial to public order," or threatened public tranquillity. He might be arrested forthwith and detained in prison for a period varying from two weeks to two years, and then by a stroke of the pen be deported, forcibly, to any part of the empire and kept there under police surveillance for from one to ten years. He could not protest or seek to defend himself. The same impenetrable secrecy was maintained as in the dungeons of the Spanish Inquisition. Not a whisper reached him of the causes of his arrest; he might not examine the witnesses who accused him or supported the charge against him. He must not call upon friends to speak of his loyalty and good character;

he was perfectly helpless and altogether at the mercy of the authorities, and even his nearest relatives were in ignorance of his whereabouts or what happened to him. They could not help him or must not if they would.

1. The Russian word is "neblagonadiozhny" and means literally, "of whom nothing good can be expected," and the expression has been given a very wide interpretation. Young people who read certain forbidden books or join forbidden societies for the ventilation of certain principles are deemed untrustworthy.

The power to send people into exile thus arbitrarily was vested in petty authorities, officers of gendarmerie, subordinate police officials, or mere executive orders countersigned by the minister of the interior and approved by the Czar. There is nothing new in this system. The people of Russia, from noble to serf, have never enjoyed the semblance of liberty; the Russian bureaucracy has wielded the unlimited power delegated to it by the autocratic Czar, and from the beginning of the eighteenth century twenty different classes of officials could employ "administrative methods" as a substitute for judicial process. The right was vested in governors, vice-governors, chiefs of police, and provincial bureaus, ecclesiastical authorities and landed proprietors. In addition to the power to send into exile, these various authorities could at their discretion confiscate property, brand, inflict torture and flog with the knout. Village communes had also the power to order the removal by exile of members who were worthless and ill-conducted, of whom their fellows were anxious to get rid.

Innumerable cases of oppression and injustice are on record of which a few may be cited. One of the most flagrant was that of Constantine Staniukovich, who was the son of a Russian admiral. He had been in the navy but had a fondness for literature and became a writer of plays and novels condemned by the censor as of "pernicious tendency." But he continued to write and finally became the proprietor of a magazine. He was seized without warning and locked up in the fortress of St. Peter and St. Paul. His wife, who was at Baden Baden, heard nothing of his arrest, and found when she returned to St. Petersburg that he had mysteriously disappeared. She learned, after diligent inquiry, that he was in prison, and that his letters had been secretly tampered with, his offence being a correspondence through the post with a well-known Russian revolutionist residing in Switzerland. At length, after a long imprisonment, he was exiled by administrative process to Tomsk for three years. His magazine was discontinued by his absence and he was financially ruined. Neither wealth nor a high social position could save him from arbitrary treatment.

Another literary man, M. Berodin, was banished to Yakutsk, close to the Arctic Circle, because the manuscript of an article deemed "dangerous" was found in his house in St. Petersburg by the police. This was a spare copy of an article he had written for the *Annals of the Fatherland*, which had been accepted but had not appeared. When he was on his way to Eastern Siberia to expiate this horrible offence, the incriminated article was passed by the censor and actually published without objection in the same magazine, and without the alteration or omission of a single line. The exile read his own article, for which he had suffered, in the far-off place of his confinement.

The most monstrous instances of high handed proceedings are recorded. One unfortunate gentleman was exiled because he was suspected of an intention to put himself in an illegal situation, no more than a projected change of name. Another man was exiled and sent to Siberia because he was the friend of an accused person who was waiting trial on a political charge, and of which he was in due course acquitted. But the friend of this innocent man was deemed an offender, and was sent across the frontier. Such was the chaos of injustice, accident and caprice, that errors were constantly made as to identification. When the roll of a travelling party was called, no one answered to the name of Vladimir Sidoski. A Victor Sidoski was in the ranks and was challenged to answer. "It is not my name. I am another man, I ought not to have been arrested; I am Victor, not Vladimir," was the answer. "You will do quite as well," retorted the officer. "I shall correct the name in the list." And Victor the innocent became Vladimir the prisoner. It sometimes happened that an arrest was made by mistake; the wrong man was taken and it was clearly shown, but no release followed. It was unsafe to take up the case of any victims of misusage. One lady who resented acts of manifest injustice was arrested and banished because "it was no business of hers."

A young and skilful surgeon, Dr. Bieli, was shamefully ill-treated. Two women students at a medical college in St. Petersburg had been expelled on suspicion of "untrustworthiness," and being anxious to continue their studies, had remained in the capital and had secretly become the doctor's pupils. They were without passports in an "illegal" position and should have been handed over to the police. But Dr. Bieli shielded them until their visits to his house, generally at night, attracted the attention of the police, and it was thought that some political conspiracy was in progress. Arrests followed, the fatal truth came out, and Dr. Bieli was exiled to the arctic village of Vorkhoyansk. His wife was expecting her confinement and could not go with him, but travelled after him, starting on a journey of six thousand miles to be made in the rough jolting *telyegas* and enduring endless hardships. Her health broke down and gradually her mind gave way. But she bore up until the end of her trials seemed near, when she learned that a mistake had occurred in the place of her destination and that she must traverse another three thousand miles before she reached her husband. The sudden shock was fatal;

she became violently insane and died a few months later in the prison hospital at Irkutsk.

The measure of administrative process has been defended by intelligent Russians who visit the blame upon the Nihilists and terrorists,—"a band so horribly vile that their crimes are beyond parallel." A writer in a German periodical justifies this language by denouncing the bloodthirsty recklessness of the revolutionists who have not hesitated to use the assassin's knife and dynamite bombs. To give local authorities power to banish the suspected was essential as a means of precaution, "the only possible means to counteract the nefarious doings of these dark conspirators." Admitting, however, that the decision was unfortunate and has caused unspeakable misery, he says: "From the day this power was delegated no man knows at what moment he may not be seized and cast into prison or doomed to exile."

He casts all the responsibility on the revolutionists, but in doing so, as Kennan says, puts the cart before the horse. Terrorist measures were the reply to grievous oppression. "It was administrative exile, administrative caprice, and the absence of orderly and legal methods in political cases that caused terrorism, not terrorism that necessitated official lawlessness." Already the true facts are patent and thoroughly understood by the world at large. The so-called excesses of the revolutionists have not been committed, as the champions of the Russian government would have us believe, "by bloodthirsty tigers in human form at the prompting of presumptuous fancies," but "by ordinary men and women exasperated to the pitch of desperation by administrative suppression of free speech and free thought, administrative imprisonment for years upon suspicion, administrative banishment to the arctic regions without trial, and, to crown all, administrative denial of every legal remedy and every peaceful means of redress."

Already "the whirligig of time has brought its revenges." Russia is wading through blood to the still far-off horizon which is at last dawning on a vexed and tortured people. The overthrow of despotism is approaching inevitably if slowly. The will of the people cannot be ignored or their aspirations checked and crushed by the old arbitrary methods of repression and coercion.

A whole volume might be filled with the detailed iniquities of the administrative process, which was so largely operative and so long before the oppressed people were goaded into retaliation. As far back as the early decades of the nineteenth century, statistics were gathered by a careful and industrious writer covering the period between 1827 and 1846 and showing the average number banished annually to be between three and six thousand, and the aggregate for the twenty years to be nearly eighty thousand. Beyond doubt in more recent years the numbers have steadily grown, although the exact figures are not available.

Kropotkin ably summarises the objects of exile: "Students and girls suspected of subversive ideas; writers whom it was impossible to prosecute for their writings, but who were known to be imbued with a 'dangerous spirit;' workmen who were known to have spoken against the authorities; persons who have been irreverent to some governor of a province or *ispravnik* were transported by hundreds every year." The barest denunciation and the most casual suggestion were sufficient to afford a motive.

Several young girls were condemned, not merely to exile, but to hard labour for from six to eight years for having given a socialistic pamphlet to one workman. A child of fourteen became a penal colonist for shouting aloud that it was a shame to condemn people to death for nothing.

A flagrant case was that of M. Annenkov, a landed proprietor, who proposed the health of the governor at a banquet given him by the nobility of Kursk. At the end he was bold enough to remark that he greatly hoped his excellency would devote more time to the affairs of the province. The following week a *tarantas* containing two gensdarmes stopped at his door; he was arrested, was forbidden to bid his wife farewell, and was conveyed as a prisoner to a distant part. Only after six months and the most urgent representations of influential friends was he again set free.

In the last decade of the reign of Alexander II, between 1870 and 1880, administrative exile was employed with unprecedented recklessness and the most consummate indifference to personal rights. Unlimited discretionary powers were vested in governors of provinces. General Todleben, in Odessa, banished all of the "untrustworthy" class without inquiry or discrimination, and sent into exile every one whose loyalty to the existing government was even doubtful. It was enough to be registered as a "suspect" on the books of the secret police, or to have been accused, even anonymously, of political disaffection. Parents who had the most honourable record of unblemished loyalty were exiled because their children had become revolutionists; schoolboys were exiled because they were acquainted with some of the disaffected and had failed to report the fact to the police; teachers were exiled for circulating copies of a harmless magazine; members of provincial assemblies, who claimed the right to petition the Czar for redress of grievances, were sent across the frontier; and university students, who had been tried and acquitted of a political offence, were re-arrested and exiled by administrative process,—all in violation of the most elementary principles of justice.

The majority of the administrative exiles were political prisoners, but all politicals were not let off with simple banishment. A considerable number of political offenders were sentenced to hard labour and also to penal exile. They did not live apart but were incorporated with the common-law criminals and subjected to precisely the same irksome treatment; they were equally deprived of civil rights, and could never count upon freedom absolute and unconditional. A few might in the long run be allowed to return to European Russia, at the intercession and with the guarantee of influential friends, but endless exile was generally their portion and a hard hand-to-mouth existence, with unceasing struggles to gain bread, for when nominally free they are still under police surveillance and do not easily find the means of a livelihood. They are worse off than when prisoners, for they are granted no government allowance and must fight for every kopeck under many disadvantages.

We come thus to the large class of the *ssylny*, those simply banished, whose liberty is forfeited, although they are not actually subjected to imprisonment; and with them must be comprised the emancipists, those who have completed their penalty but are not permitted to leave Siberia. Both classes are practically prisoners, although not within four walls perhaps. Their movements are restricted, and they are still held under observation within a certain area and must observe certain stringent rules of conduct. Their condition is only a modified form of imprisonment applicable to at least half of the entire number transported to Siberia.

A code of rules has been drawn up for all whom the law condemns to exile and enforced domicile, whether at home or in far-off Siberia. The pregnant word "banishment" is carefully excluded from these rules, and police surveillance takes effect on those "assigned to definite places of residence," an expression euphemistically applied to the wildest and most remote regions of the empire. It is an obviously colourable suppression of true facts. The names of such places as the frontiers of Mongolia, the arctic province of Yakutsk, or the sub-tropical mountain districts of Central Asia are never mentioned, but there can be no mistakes as to the irksome character of the rules. It is a life of sufferance, of sometimes open arrest, and often of rigorously curtailed freedom of movement. The exile must remain where he is planted; to move his quarters he must give notice and obtain the consent of the police, to whom he must constantly report himself. His chosen place of residence is liable to visitation and search at any time of the day or night, and anything it contains may be removed; his correspondence, all letters and telegrams, inward and outward, may be read or withheld at all times.

The manner of the exile's daily life is laid down with great minuteness, and the nature of his employments specified, chiefly in the negative sense. He cannot hold any position in the service of the state; he must do no clerical work for any society or institution; he must not promote, or serve with any company; he cannot act as curator of any museum; he must not give lectures or impart instruction as a schoolmaster; he must not take any part in any theatricals, and is forbidden generally to exercise any public activity. He may not embark in any photographic or literary occupation; may not deal in books, must not keep a tea house or grog shop, or trade in intoxicating liquors. He shall not appear or plead in court except on behalf of himself and his near relations, nor without special permission may he act as physician, accoucheur, apothecary or chemist. The penalty of contravening any of these regulations is imprisonment for terms varying from three days to one month. Exiles without means are granted a meagre allowance from the treasury, but it is withdrawn if they fail to obtain employment through bad conduct or laziness. The difficulty of getting a living under so many restrictions is not considered.

The exile's life is full of irksome conditions. When, after a nearly interminable journey, he reaches his "definite domicile," he must find his own residence with some reluctant householder who does not care to shelter a presumably dangerous political, subject at all times of the day or night to police visitation; and, moreover, the householder is expected to spy upon his tenant and report any suspicious circumstance. When at length he overcomes these irritating and causeless objections and rents a bare room, he has to settle the question of daily subsistence. His wife and family he has left behind in Russia, probably destitute, while he is here in Siberia without means, and with little hope of being able to secure them. He falls back on the government grant, no more than twelve shillings a month, and finds that it is utterly insufficient to provide him with the commonest necessaries of life. Rent, coarse food, meat, rye flour, a few eggs, "brick" tea and a little cheap tobacco exhaust his allowance and leave a substantial deficit, and this without spending a kopeck on washing, kerosene or medicine.

Naturally the exile seeks to supplement his inadequate income. His position is nearly hopeless. Possibly he has had the best education, is a graduate of the university, knows several languages, and is a skilful surgeon or practised physician. He does not, of course, expect to find in the wilds of Siberia as many openings for his trained intelligence as in St. Petersburg or Moscow, but surely there is room for an expert penman, a good accountant, a competent teacher, a fair musician? Yet he seems to have no chance to earn a few rubles, a few kopecks even, day by day. The regulations, quoted above, close every avenue, debar him from every employment but ordinary manual labour. He has never learned any handicraft; he cannot work as carpenter, shoemaker, wheelwright or blacksmith; he has no capital and cannot go into trade; he must not engage himself as driver or teamster, for he cannot leave the village to which he has been assigned. There is nothing left for him except to dig, but there is not an inch of land for him to cultivate. All the ground in the neighbourhood belongs to the village commune and has been already

CHAPTER IV
THE OSTROG AT OMSK

Centre of exile system at Omsk—Dostoyevski—His famous book "Recollections of the Dead House" based on his experiences in this Ostrog—Description of the prison and its heterogeneous inmates—Detestable character of an ex-noble—His attempted escape with another convict—Another well-born criminal of very different character—His industry and skill with his hands—The prison routine—Food—Extra delicacies could be obtained—Passion for gambling—Various devices for indulging it—Method of smuggling strong drink into the Ostrog—Drunken carousals—Gazin, the vodka seller—His history and atrocious crimes—Dostoyevski narrowly escapes being murdered by him.

In the early decades of the nineteenth century the exile system centred chiefly at Omsk, an ancient military post situated on the junction of the rivers Om and Irtysh. A place of arms had been erected here in 1719 to strengthen the Russian dominion among the nomads of the Asiatic Steppes. This was replaced by a formidable fortress and became a chief post on the Siberian boundary line. A large town sprang up around it, which grew into the headquarters of local administration, and was long the residence of the governor-general of Western Siberia.

Just outside the ramparts of the fortress stood a wooden prison, enclosed by a high stockade, which has an interesting penal history, having served for long years as a base and starting point for the convict exiles on their eastward march. The prison population constantly numbered about eight hundred and it was the place of durance for several remarkable prisoners. One of the greatest of Russian novelists, Dostoyevski, based his famous book, "Reminiscences of the Dead House" on his personal experiences in this old *ostrog*.[2] He was one of the early "politicals" who were subjected to the same régime as the common-law prisoner or ordinary gaol-bird, and he suffered four years as a hard-labour convict at Omsk. His offence was being involved in the Petrachevski affair in 1849, and with him in Omsk was the poet Dirov, who suffered a like term of four years for the same reason.

2. The *ostrog* was the name given to the stockaded entrenchment or rude fort built by the Cossack invaders of Siberia in the old days. As prisoners were confined more and more in these forts, the word *ostrog* came to define a place of durance, and is now applied to all local prisons in Siberia, and provincial lock-ups. The prison had disappeared when Kennan looked for it on his visit to Omsk. New buildings have been erected on the site.

Dostoyevski's treatment, having regard to his offence, was a disgrace to civilisation, and it is satisfactory to know that intelligent Russian officials to-day are heartily ashamed of the episode. A full account of its enormities has been since written by a fellow prisoner named Rozhnovski, and was published in the Tiflis newspaper, *Kavkaz*. He was at the mercy of harsh taskmasters, endured the severest discipline, wore irons always and the prisoners' dress, and was twice flogged. The first corporal punishment he received was for complaining in the name of the other prisoners of filthy foreign matter floating in the daily soup, and the second was for saving the life of a comrade from drowning, in direct defiance of his officer's order to do nothing of the kind. The second "execution" was so terrible that the victim was taken up for dead; he lay insensible for so long that he was afterward nicknamed the "deceased."

Never have the inner life and history of a Russian prison of that epoch—the middle of the nineteenth century—been so thoroughly explored and exposed as by the gifted writer, Dostoyevski. He draws on his own experience, speaking at first hand from his personal knowledge. He knew exactly what imprisonment meant, for he had been through it, constantly subjected to its irksome restraints and almost intolerable conditions. He had learned to habituate himself to its laws and penalties; to endure the most acute discomforts; to face with patient resignation the endless vista of the slow moving years, continually tortured and tormented by suffering and the complete absence of all that tends to brighten life and make it bearable. He had ample opportunities for studying and observing the convicts with whom he was so long obliged to consort. He draws them with photographic exactitude. He observed, and has effectively reproduced their traits, thoughts, feelings and inner nature. He saw them at their best and at their worst; he noted the generous emotions that sometimes swayed them, the evil passions that more often possessed them. He can do justice to the sympathy and compassion lavished on suffering comrades and reprobates; to the envy, hatred and uncharitableness constantly exhibited when moved by jealousy or consumed with temper and overmastering desire for revenge. The daily life of a Siberian place of durance at that time is brought before us with striking force: its generally wearisome monotony, to which severe toil is a welcome break; the petty, pitiful recreations enjoyed often at the risk of punishment; the vices of drunkenness and gambling, strictly forbidden although constantly indulged in; the gormandising at Christmas and other festivals. He describes the ambitious theatrical entertainment given in the convict barrack room, when the convicts, despite the difficulties raised by discipline and the dearth of means, produced a striking performance.

The old prison at Omsk was situated at the end of the citadel just under the ramparts. It was surrounded by a high palisade of stakes buried deep in the ground, enclosing a court-yard two hundred feet long by one hundred and fifty feet broad. A great gate in the stockade guarded by sentries gave detailed to execute some repairs at a distant military barrack at that time empty of troops. In the middle of the job, the corporal took off his two prisoners, ostensibly to fetch some tools from another shop. Kulikov, with a wink, added that he would bring back some vodka, but the liquor never arrived nor the prisoners. They had gone into the town to a secure hiding place, where they changed their clothes and got rid of their irons and lay by waiting for a quiet moment to escape after the first excitement had blown over.

Their disappearance was not realised for some hours. The hue and cry was then raised and a thorough search instituted. The authorities were most unhappy, for stringent regulations had been neglected; the convicts should have been guarded by at least two men apiece and not allowed to come and go as they pleased. Inside the prison everything was turned upside down, and the prisoners were repeatedly searched and cross-questioned. The guards were doubled in the prison and beyond it, expresses were despatched to all police stations around, and mounted Cossacks beat up all the surrounding country. It was comparatively open ground; the forests were at some distance and no cover was at hand. At the end of a week the prison-breakers were recaptured in a village only seventy versts distant, and were brought back to the *ostrog*, chained hand and foot. Severe flogging was the certain retribution for attempted escape; Kulikov was adjudged by a court-martial to suffer fifteen hundred lashes, and the originator of the plot five hundred, but as he was consumptive, he was excused from a portion of the punishment by the doctor of the prison.

Another well-born convict was of a character so different that he merits a detailed description. His name was Akim Akimych, and he had been an officer who, when serving as a sub-lieutenant in the Caucasus, had put a small tributary prince to death. He was in command of a petty fort in the mountains, and his neighbour, the prince, made a night attack upon it, meaning to burn it about his ears, but the enterprise failed. Akimych pretended not to be aware of his real assailant, and invited the prince to come and pay him a friendly visit. A great show was made; the garrison was paraded and the guest royally entertained. After dinner Akimych took the prince severely to task, reproached him with his treachery, and shot him. He at once reported this summary action to his superior officer, who placed him under arrest and brought him to trial by court-martial, which sentenced him to death; but the penalty was commuted to twelve years' imprisonment in Siberia. He bowed submissively to his hard fate, but defended his conduct. "The prince had tried to burn my fort. What was I to do? Was I to thank him for it?" he asked pertinently.

Akimych was a strange medley of opposite qualities. In aspect tall and much emaciated, in temper obstinate, and not very well educated, he was excessively argumentative and particular about the accuracy of details. He was very excitable, very quarrelsome, easily offended and most sensitive. The other convicts, who generally despised the nobles, laughed at him when not afraid of him, and he claimed at once a footing of perfect equality with them, which he maintained by insulting them, calling them thieves and vagabonds and, if necessary, beating them. He had a keen appreciation of justice and fair play and would interfere in anything he thought unjustifiable, whether it concerned him or not. He was esteemed for his straightforward ways and not a little for his cleverness and skill with his fingers.

Akimych could do almost anything; he was an adept at all trades, was a good cobbler and boot-maker, an excellent locksmith, a painter, and a carver and gilder. These trades he had acquired in the prison by merely watching and imitating his fellow workmen. One handicraft at which he laboured assiduously was the making of variegated paper lanterns, which he sold at a good price in the town, from where orders came in abundance. He also manufactured baskets and toys, so that he was never without money, which he spent in the purchase of shirts, pillows, tea and extra food. Akimych laboured methodically and regularly until a late hour in the night, and then put away his tools, unfolded his mattress, repeated his prayers and turned in to sleep the sleep of the just.

After the night closing, the interior of the barrack became a hive of industry. It looked like a large workshop. Strictly speaking, private labour was not permitted, but this was winked at as the only means of keeping the convicts quiet during the long hours of a winter's evening. They were then quite safe from interruption. During the day, some of the under officers might come in prying and poking about, and the convicts had to be on their guard. As soon as the gates were padlocked, however, everyone sat down in his place and began his work. The interior of the barrack was suddenly lighted up; every man had his own candle and his wooden candlestick, and they all set to work without fear of interruption. Work was not exactly forbidden, but the possession of tools was, and the order was secretly evaded. Each man hungered for the earnings of this private labour, a few coppers, and that it apparently was allowed in this Russian *ostrog*, unlike prisons elsewhere, was a tangible boon, a certain small compensation for the loss of liberty. Money might be spent, surreptitiously, in buying tobacco and drink, both strictly prohibited, but all the more sweet because indulgence in them was forbidden. Besides, if not quickly expended, the money might be confiscated in the constant and minute searches made. The prisoners were being continually "turned over," and ruthlessly deprived of any money that might be found. The only safe plan was to entrust the cash to one old man, who was strictly honest and extremely cunning at concealment. One of his hiding places was in the stockade at some height, where the stump end of a branch protruded;

- 54 -

it was removable, and within was a cavity running down to some depth. The secret was jealously guarded, for the convicts were expert thieves and without a scrap of conscience.

Dostoyevski, for the safe keeping of his small possessions, bought a small box with a lock and key. This was forced open the first night and everything was abstracted. At another time, a comrade who pretended a warm friendship, stole his pocket Bible from him, the only book he was permitted to possess, and sold it forthwith for drink. The friend had been asked to carry it into the barrack only a few yards away. On the way he met a purchaser and at once disposed of the Bible for a few kopecks. He confessed the theft the same evening, explaining that he had a sudden craving for vodka and could not resist it. When the thirst was on him he would have committed murder to gratify it. He talked of the theft as quite an ordinary incident, and when reproved was not in the least ashamed. He listened calmly, agreed that it was a very useful book and was sorry he had taken it, but in his inner heart thought the grievance was mere nonsense.

Ameliorations of this life might be secured (for money); recreations were possible, though they were mostly vicious, and amusements even might be surreptitiously enjoyed or winked at by the authorities. Human nature is so constituted that it becomes habituated to anything, and the inmates of the *ostrog* learned to endure its worst evils, and, except for the pain of personal chastisement or the acute sufferings engendered by disease, they spent their weary, unlovely days with dogged, callous indifference.

At daybreak every morning a drum beaten near the principal entrance roused all from the last refreshing sleep obtained in the small hours when mosquitoes and more loathsome insects had desisted from their attacks. The convicts rose from their plank beds to the music of clanking leg irons, their inseparable companions, and, trembling with cold as the icy air rushed in through the unbarred open gates, gathered around the water pails, took water into their mouths and washed their faces with their hands. These pails had been filled the night before by appointed orderlies. Personal cleanliness is not entirely neglected by the peasant class in Russia, nor even by convicts, and the periodical vapour bath was greatly appreciated. The orderlies, like the cooks, were chosen by the convicts themselves from among their numbers; they did not work with the rest, but, as elsewhere, attended to the washing of the floors, the condition of camp bedsteads, and the provision of water for ablutions and for drinking.

After roll-call, the entire number proceeded to the kitchen, where the first meal of the day was eaten in common. The convicts, in their sheepskin overcoats, received their ration of black bread in their parti-coloured, round, peakless caps, from the cooks who had cut up the loaves for them with the "rascal," the prison knife, which was the only weapon permitted in the place. As many as could find room, sat grouped around the tables and laughed noisily; some soaked pieces of bread in the cups of sour tea, *kvas*, in front of them; others drank the tea they were permitted to provide for themselves. This privilege was extended to food generally, and the convicts who could pay for it bought their own, which was cooked in the public kitchen and substituted for the ordinary prison fare. Osip, one of the prison cooks, or "cook maids" as they were commonly called, prepared the food, which was purchased in the town market by the old soldiers who were attached to the prison to watch over the general discipline and good order of the place. They were good-natured veterans, always ready to run messages and purvey to the needs of the prisoners.

Dostoyevski at first could not stomach the regulation cabbage soup, but eventually overcame his repugnance. Meanwhile, he had his own private table, which cost him no more than a couple of rubles monthly, and he had a morsel of roast meat every day, cooked by Osip in some mysterious fashion that was never divulged. Osip was practically his servant, and was paid regular wages. Suchilov was another who acted as personal attendant, boiled the tea-urn, performed commissions, mended clothes and greased the great-boots four times monthly. Suchilov was an "exchange," a convict who had changed places with another of longer sentence, assuming the punishment for a sum in cash. He was a poor devil, always impecunious, ready for any menial occupation and regularly employed as a lookout man by the gamblers when at play. For five kopecks a night he kept watch in the passage in absolute darkness and in temperatures varying between winter cold and extreme summer heat, to give alarm if any superior officer paid a night visit, for when caught at cards the convicts would pay the penalty with their backs,—all would be soundly flogged. But the terrors of corporal punishment did not conquer the passion for play. There were always men who had the wherewithal,—a small piece of carpet as board, or "deck," a candle and a greasy pack of well-thumbed cards. The fortunate possessor of these necessaries received fifteen kopecks for their use. The game played was chiefly *gorka*, or "three leaves," a pure game of chance, and it was continued until far into the night, often until the break of dawn, or within a few minutes of the morning drum. The stakes were for copper coins, but relatively large sums were won and lost.

The passion for gambling was deeply rooted and still consumes the Russian prisoner. Among the exiles travelling in pain and anguish across the Siberian continent, it had such a hold that men would risk their last farthing of the meagre allowance issued for daily rations, and if unlucky, would be obliged to go hungry or depend entirely upon charity. Cards were generally forthcoming, but when none were on hand, various ingenious devices were put in practice on the road. One was to spread an overcoat, or soiled linen foot-robe, on the floor of the prison room, and the game was to guess the exact number of fleas that would jump upon it in a given length of time, and back the opinion with a wager. Another plan was to chalk two small circles, one within the other, on one of the sleeping platforms, *nary*, and place a number of vermin in the inner circle. Then the player would bet on the animal he believed would first cross the line into the outer circle. These unsavoury methods were also pursued in the old English war prison at Dartmoor.

A craving for strong drink was constantly exhibited, and strange to say, could generally be gratified. A large business was done in smuggling spirits into the *ostrog*. The trade was hazardous but proportionately lucrative. It was undertaken by the convict who was ignorant of any handicraft or too idle to acquire one. His capital was his back, which he was ready to lay bare to the lash if detected in the nefarious traffic, and he must possess a small amount of cash to expend in the vodka. This money he entrusted to some resident in the town, soldier, shopkeeper or free labourer, who brought it up to the prison and concealed it in some hiding place agreed upon outside the gates, on the works to which the convict had access. The stuff paid contribution in transit, and was well watered, but the convict buyer had no redress and took what he could get. With the fluid a length of bullock's intestines was left, which, when washed, was filled with the vodka and wound around the waist of the convict about to introduce it into the prison. The carrier ran the risk of detection when searched, but he had a bribe convenient to slip into the hand of the corporal at the gate, and he might have the good luck to escape observation. If he failed, he paid the penalty of a severe flogging. On the other hand, the forbidden liquor might win through, and the convict dealer would then have a supply of stuff for the convict customers among his comrades.

As soon as enough money had been earned or stolen, the time was ripe for a carouse, a drunken holiday, when the whole sum, painfully put together, kopeck by kopeck, was lavished in one glorious burst of self-indulgence. The man was resolved to enjoy himself. "These days of rejoicing had been looked forward to long beforehand," says Dostoyevski. "He had dreamed of them during the endless winter nights, during his hardest labour, and the prospect had supported him under his severest trials. The dawn of this day so impatiently awaited has just appeared ... accordingly he takes his savings to the drink seller who at first gives him vodka, almost pure, but gradually as the bottle gets more and more empty, he fills it up with water. It may be imagined that many glasses and much money are required before the convict is drunk. But, as he is out of the habit, the little alcohol remaining in the liquid easily intoxicates, he drinks all he can get, pledges or sells all his own clothes and then those belonging to the government. When he has made away with his last shirt, he lies down in a drunken sleep and wakes up next day with a bad headache." Then he began again to work for many weary months and amass the means for another debauch.

As for the drink seller, he made his profit to be spent in adding to his stock in trade. But this time he drank it himself. Enough of trade, he would have a little amusement. Accordingly he ate, drank and paid for a little music, and kept it up for several days until his money was gone, unless, indeed, misfortune overtook him. It might be that some of the officers had noticed his condition, and he was dragged before the major in the orderly room, where he was arraigned, convicted and punished with the rods. Then he shook himself like a beaten dog, and after a few days resumed his trade as drink seller. Detection was not frequent, for the convicts would do all they could to shield a man under the influence of drink. Russians have generally a sympathy for drunkenness. Among convicts it amounted to worship. The condition implied aristocratic distinction, and the man in his cups swaggered and showed himself off with a great assumption of superiority.

The phrase "pay for a little music" needs explanation. A convict in funds and half drunk was in the habit of hiring a musician to make a greater show. There was one who had been a bandsman in the army and who possessed a fiddle which he was ready to play for anyone who paid him, and he would follow his employer about from barrack to barrack, grinding out dance tunes with his utmost strength and skill. His face showed his disgust and boredom, but if he slackened his arm he was roughly reminded to go on more briskly and earn his wage properly.

This love of ostentatious extravagance found other outlets. Drinking to excess was not the only form of self-indulgence. Gormandising was another. The convict when in funds would treat himself to a fine feast, the materials for which were brought in from the town by the old soldier go-between above mentioned. The occasion chosen was always on some religious festival and began by the convict placing a wax candle before the holy image or *ikon* in its honoured corner. Then he would dress himself with extreme care and sit down to dinner in state. He would devour course after course,—fish, meat, patties,—gorging himself quite alone. It was seldom that the selfish creature invited any comrade to share his repast.

A fondness for new clothes was very noticeable in the prosperous convict, and he was not forbidden to substitute the garments of his choice for the prison uniform, which consisted of a coarse shirt, long gray dressing gown, loose drawers and peakless cap. Their taste in clothes ran to gay waistcoats and fancy trousers, coloured shirts, and belts with metal clasps. On Sundays the dandies in the prison put on their best clothes to strut about the barrack yard. But the glory of display soon yielded to the temptation to buy drink and make a little cash. The evening of the very day on which they were first worn the smart clothes would disappear, sold or pledged to the convict pawnbrokers, ever ready for business.

Usury was followed in the *ostrog* quite as a profession. Money was borrowed on all kinds of pledges, often upon articles of equipment, the property of the government. There was no good faith about the transaction. When the money had been advanced, the borrower would go at once and inform the authorities that goods belonging to the state were in the unlawful possession of the usurer, who was forthwith obliged to give them up and accept his loss with the usual penalty of the lash.

A notable specimen of the dealers in vodka was a convict named Gazin, a terrible creature of gigantic proportions and enormous bodily strength. "A more ferocious and more monstrous creature could not exist. He was a Tartar with an enormous and deformed head, like a gigantic spider of the size of a man." The strangest reports were current about him. He was said to have been at one time a soldier; to have been repeatedly exiled, and to have as often escaped only to be recaptured. He had been guilty of the most frightful crimes. He took a delight in killing small children, whom he attracted to some deserted spot, terrified into convulsions, tortured horribly and then murdered. In the prison, however, he seldom exhibited his worst traits. He was generally quiet in demeanour, rarely quarrelsome, and careful to avoid disputes, having too great a contempt for his companions and too good an opinion of himself. His face was not without intelligence, but cruel and derisive in expression like his smile.

Gazin was the richest of all the vodka sellers, and at regular intervals used his stock in trade for self indulgence. Twice yearly he got completely drunk and when in his cups displayed all his brutal ferocity. As he grew more and more excited, he assailed his comrades with gibes, invectives and venomous satire long since prepared. When quite intoxicated, he waxed furious and, flourishing his knife, truculently rushed at some one to kill him. Then a combined attack was made upon him, and he was disarmed after he had been made unconscious by blows upon the pit of the stomach. When well beaten, he was wrapped up in his pelisse and thrown on to his camp bed to sleep off the effects of drink. On every occasion exactly the same thing occurred; the prisoners knew what would happen as did Gazin himself. This went on for years until his physical energy began to fail; he weakened, complained of illness, and frequently became a patient in hospital, where he was well treated and in due course died.

Gazin, in one of his drunken bouts, fell foul of Dostoyevski and nearly murdered him. He came into the kitchen one day, followed by his fiddler, and staggered up to a table where our author sat with a friend or two drinking. He smiled maliciously and asked with an insolent jeer how they could afford to buy tea. No answer was given, as any contradiction would have maddened him. Their continued silence had just the same effect. "You must have money," he went on, "a great deal of money; but tell me, are you sent to hard labour to drink tea? Please tell me; I should like to know." Still there was no reply. He trembled and grew livid with rage and looking round for some weapon of offence, seized the heavy bread box and rushed at Dostoyevski, raising it over his head. Death seemed imminent for one and all when a diversion was fortunately created by a voice crying, "Gazin! they have stolen your vodka." The miscreant instantly dropped the box and ran off to recover his treasure. It was never known whether there had been any theft, or whether the words were invented as a stratagem to save the lives threatened.

The vodka seller was in his glory at Christmas time, when there were great festivities and a drunken orgy was in progress with the tacit permission of the authorities. Gazin kept sober until toward the end of the celebration. He stood by the side of his camp bedstead, beneath which he had concealed his store of drink, after bringing it from his customary hiding place deep buried under the snow in the barrack yard. "He smiled knowingly when he saw his customers arrive in crowds. He drank nothing himself; he waited for that till the last day when he had emptied the pockets of his comrades," who degenerated into the wildest excesses, singing, laughing and crying by turns, patrolling the barrack room in bands, and striking the strings of their *balalaiki* or native guitars.

To drink to excess was the chief way to find an outlet for rejoicing; it was also the means of deadening the hideous anticipation of acute and inevitable pain. A convict sentenced to be flogged invariably contrived to swallow the largest possible dose of spirits beforehand, often a long time ahead and at a fabulous price. A certain conviction prevailed that a drunken man suffered less from the plet or "the stick" than a sober one in the full possession of his faculties. In one case, an ex-soldier awaiting punishment infused a quantity of snuff into a bottle of vodka and drank it off at once. He was seized with violent convulsions, vomited blood, and was taken to hospital unconscious. His lungs had been hopelessly affected, phthisis declared itself and he soon died of consumption.

found who for a kopeck or two were willing to lay strokes on the heated flesh of the employers with birch rods of twisted twigs. It must have been a hideous scene, a great mass of commingled humanity in a state of half intoxication, shouting and shrieking at the top of their voices. The steam grew thicker and thicker until all were soaked and saturated with it, and their bodies became scarlet in the intolerably burning and overheated atmosphere.

The *ostrog* at Omsk contained a number of widely differing types, embracing many classes of crime, the most heinous as well as venial offences. All classes and many nationalities of the widespread Russian Empire were represented; well-bred nobles, degraded from their rank and sent to herd with serfs and peasants, and "old believers" from little Russia, insurgent Poles, mutinous soldiers sentenced by court-martial for desertion and grave acts of insubordination, mountaineers from the Caucasus exiled for brigandage, and Mahometans from Daghestan who lay in wait for passing caravans and pillaged them and assassinated the merchant travellers. There were murderers in many varieties; Cain who killed slowly and deliberately with deep malice and forethought, and the slayer moved to murder by swiftly risen, passionate impulse in a sudden irresistible access of fury. Thieves of all sorts abounded; petty pilferers and robbers on a grand scale; the wandering tramps or *brodyagi* who had escaped from durance to range the woods and steal from all they met. There were also many smugglers, long trained and practised in the traffic, who clung with great attachment to the business and who were constantly engaged in the clandestine introduction of spirits into the prison.

The story of one murderer, Petrov, exhibits a curious and somewhat uncommon character. He had been a soldier and had suddenly revolted at the ill-usage of his colonel who struck him one day on parade. It was not the first time he had been beaten, for the personal chastisement of their men was by no means uncommon with Russian officers, but on this occasion Petrov would not tamely submit, and retaliated by stabbing the colonel to the heart. It was said of him in prison that when the spirit moved him, nothing would stop him; he was capable of anything, and he would kill a man without the smallest hesitation or without showing the slightest remorse. The evil temper in him was easily aroused and was then ungovernable. Once he was sentenced to be whipped for some minor offence, no small punishment certainly, and he resolved not to submit to it. He had been previously flogged more than once and had borne his punishment calmly and philosophically. But this time he considered that he was innocent and wrongfully sentenced. He meant to resist, even to go so far as to kill the governor, if necessary, sooner than yield. This major-governor was a much dreaded being, a tyrannical disciplinarian, with lynx-like eyes for the detection of any irregularity; he was commonly called by the convicts "the man with eight eyes." His severe method had generally the effect of irritating his charges, naturally ill-tempered and irascible men.

Petrov made no secret of his fell purpose, and it was known throughout the prison that when called up for punishment he would make an end of the major. He had successfully concealed a sharp-pointed shoemaker's awl, which he held ready in his hand as he was marched under escort to the place of execution. The prisoners, in breathless anticipation of what they might see, clung close to the stockade, peering through the interstices, for they believed the major's last hour had come. But the major, quite ignorant of his impending doom, had suddenly decided not to witness the flogging, and drove home in his carriage leaving his lieutenant to superintend the punishment parade. "God has saved him," ejaculated the convicts piously, and Petrov submitted to his ordeal without a murmur. His anger was against the major and it had disappeared when the object was removed.

On another occasion, he had quarrelled with a comrade over the possession of a worthless piece of rag. They disputed with great violence and a collision seemed inevitable. Suddenly Petrov turned pale, his lips trembled, growing blue and bloodless, his respiration became difficult, and slowly he approached his antagonist step by step—he always walked with naked feet—while a deathlike stillness around succeeded the noisy chatter of the other convicts in the yard. The man he threatened awaited him tremblingly and suddenly blanched and gave in by throwing the cloth of contention at his adversary, using the most horrible and insulting language toward him.

This Petrov was a man of contradictory traits. In person he was of short stature, agile and strongly built, with a pleasant face, a bold expression, white regular teeth and an agreeable voice. He seemed quite young, no more than thirty, although he was fully forty years of age. He always appeared absent-minded and had a habit of looking into the distance over and beyond near objects. An attentive listener, joining with animation in the talk, he would suddenly become silent, oppressed, as it were, with disturbing thoughts. He was deemed a most resolute character and inspired the utmost awe in every one, as capable of anything if the caprice seized him; ready to murder any one out of hand without hesitation, and never deterred by the dread of subsequent remorse. He generally showed tact and forbearance in his relations with others, spoke to them civilly and was not easily roused or annoyed.

Sirotkin was another type of ex-soldier who had found military discipline insufferable and was resolved to escape from it at any cost. All went wrong with him; every one was harsh and cruel and he was forever being punished, and sobbing as if broken-hearted in some remote corner. One dark night when on sentry duty he was so unutterably sad that he placed the muzzle of the assistance of the convicts themselves. Every one supplemented the daily ration with choice morsels privately purchased out of hard-earned savings. But no one tasted food until the priest arrived with cross and holy water; a small table had been prepared for him with a holy image on it, and before it a lamp was burning. After he had conducted the service, the pre-Christmas fast ended, and the feast began by the permission of the commandant, who had visited the barrack formally and tasted the cabbage soup, but had made no remark about the additional delicacies provided and which were now brought in to be greedily devoured.

The scene presently degenerated into an orgy. Faces became flushed with drink and good cheer; the *balalaiki*, or banjos, were produced; the fiddler, paid by a convivial convict, played lively dance music. The conversation became more and more animated and more and more noisy, but the dinner ended without great disorder. Later, drunkenness was general; it was no offence that day, and even the officers, who made the regulation visits, paid no attention. The antics of the intoxicated were an amusing spectacle to most. But a few of the more orderly and right-thinking showed their disapproval. The "old believer" from Starodub climbed up to his favourite perch on top of the stove and fervently prayed for the rest of the day. The sight of these excesses was exceedingly painful to him. The Mahometan prisoners took no part in the revels; they looked on with much curiosity and manifest disgust. The youth Nourra, already mentioned, shook his head crying, "Aman, Aman. Alas! Alas! It is an offence to Allah!" The Jew, Isaiah Fomich, declined to join in a celebration commemorating an offence committed by his co-religionists, and to show his contempt for Christ, lighted a candle and went to work in a favourite corner.

As the day passed, reckless self-indulgence gradually increased, but the general drunkenness and debauchery began to lapse into wearisome depression. Men who had been convulsed with uproarious laughter became maudlin and dropped into some out of the way spot, weeping bitter tears; others, pale and sickly, tottered about, seeking quarrels with all whom they met. Old differences were revived; disputes soon developed into personal conflicts; frequently two of the men would come to blows as to which should stand treat to the other. The whole spectacle was insupportable, nauseating and repulsive. The great festival, which should have passed with so much delight, ended in dejection and disappointment. The convicts, drunken or sober, alike dropped down on their camp beds and slept heavily.

In some countries prisoners have been permitted to find relief in theatrical performances. It was so in the Spanish presidios, and here in the old Russian *ostrog* a dramatic entertainment, on a most ambitious scale, was a feature of the Christmas holidays. A convict company was organised very secretly; it was always uncertain whether the major would consent, and all was kept from his knowledge until the last moment. The rehearsals were quite private; the names of the plays were unknown, or how the costumes and scenery were to be obtained. The stage was created in a space cleared in the centre of the barrack, and could be put up and taken down in a quarter of an hour. The moving spirit was one Bakluchin, who had been a soldier in Riga, and had murdered his rival, a German, whom he had caught paying addresses to his fiancée and who was preferred by her. This Bakluchin, who was thirty years old, was of lofty stature, with a frank, determined countenance, but good-natured and generally popular. He had the comedian's knack of changing his face in comic imitation of any passer-by, and convulsed all who saw him. As the projected performance took place, Bakluchin swelled with ill-concealed importance and boasted of the success he would achieve. He went about declaiming portions of his part and amusing everybody by anticipation.

Two popular pieces were chosen for performance, plays from an old book, preserved by memory in the traditions of the prison. Many of the "properties," too, had been handed down, carefully concealed in secret places for years. One of them, the curtain, which was a work of art, was composed of numerous scraps of cloth sewed together, such as the linen of old shirts, bandages, and underwear; even pieces of strong paper were added to fill in empty spaces; and on the surface was painted in oil a landscape with trees and ponds of flowers. This curtain delighted the convicts and shared the first applause with the orchestra of eight instruments,—two violins, three banjos, two guitars and a tambourine. The musicians played well, and the tunes were all original and distinctive.

The audience, before the curtain rose, crowded and crushed into the narrow theatre, wild with suppressed excitement. Two benches were placed immediately in front of the stage, which was lighted with candle ends. These seats, with one or two chairs, were for the officers who might deign to be present,—the overseers, clerks, directors of works and engineers. Behind stood the convicts respectfully, row after row. Some were posted on the camp beds or had climbed up on the porcelain stove, and every face glowed with delight, a strange look of infinite contentment and unmixed pleasure shining on these scarred and branded countenances so generally dark and forbidding. Everyone was dressed in his best, his short sheepskin pelisse, in spite of the suffocating heat, and each face was damp with perspiration. Everyone was there: The Tartars and Circassians, who showed a passionate delight for the theatre; Young Ali, whose childish face beamed and whose laughter was contagious; the Jew, Isaiah Fomich, who was in an ecstasy from the rising of the curtain to its fall, and rejoiced at the chance of showing off, for when the plate was passed he ostentatiously contributed the imposing sum of ten kopecks, or twopence, halfpenny.

As the play proceeded, it was received with warm applause. Cries of approbation were heard in all parts of the house. The convicts nudged each other with loud whispers, calling attention to the jokes, laughing uproariously, smacking their lips and clacking their tongues, and toward the end the gaiety reached its climax. "Imagine the convict prison," says Dostoyevski, "the chains of long years of captivity in close confinement, the bodily toil monotonous and unending, the accumulated, long protracted misery and despair, and the grim place of durance transformed on this occasion into one of light-hearted amusement where prisoners might forget their condition, dismiss the nightmare of crime and breathe freely and laugh aloud."

A comedy in prison! The convicts were in costumes altogether different from the daily garb of shame, but with the inseparable chains always obstructing. One was in female attire, wearing an old worn-out muslin dress, with neck and arms bare and a pert calico cap on his half shaven head. Another represented a gentleman of fashion in a frock coat, round hat and cloak, but his chains rattled as he strutted across the stage; one was in the full-dress but faded uniform of an aide-de-camp. There were convicts in many characters, strange and varied: a nobleman, an innkeeper, demons, a Brahmin in flowing robes. Every one was delighted when the performance ended, and the convicts separated, quite pleased to have been taken away from themselves for a brief space, full of praise for the actors and of gratitude to their superiors, who had permitted the play to be given. It was a wise concession, for the convicts made a point of conducting themselves in the most exemplary fashion.

The prisoners in the *ostrog* were fond of live animals, and if permitted, would have filled the prison with domesticated pets. They had dogs, geese, a horse and even an eagle whom they vainly sought to tame. "Bull" was a good-sized black dog with white spots, intelligent eyes and a bushy tail. He lived in the prison enclosure, slept in the courtyard, ate the waste scraps from the kitchen and had little hold on the sympathy of the men, all of whom he regarded as masters and owners. He came to greet the working parties on their return from labour, wagging his tail and looking for the caresses which he seldom got. Dostoyevski, as he tells us, was one of the first to make friends with Bull by giving him a piece of bread and patting him on the back, which pleased him greatly. "That evening, not having seen me for the whole day," says the author, "he ran up to me leaping and barking. Then he put his paws on my shoulders and looked me in the face. 'Here is a friend sent to me by destiny,' I said to myself, and during the first weeks, so full of pain, every time I returned to the barrack I hastened to fondle and make much of Bull."

Another dog was called Snow. He was a luckless creature who had been driven over and injured in the spine by the wheels of a *telyega*, "country cart."

He looked like two dogs because of the curvature of his spine, and he was mangy, with bleared eyes and a hairless tail always drooping between his hind legs. Snow was abjectly submissive to all, both men and fellow-dogs. He never barked nor made overtures, but continually turned on his back to curry favour, and received the kick of every passer without a sign of resentment, except that if hurt he would often utter one low deprecatory yelp. When surprised with a caress wholly unexpected and unusual, he quivered and whined plaintively with delight. His fate was sad and brutal; he was torn to pieces by other dogs in the ditch of the fortress.

A third dog was Kultiapka, brought in as a puppy soon after he had been born in one of the prison workshops. Bull took him under his especial protection and "fathered" and played with him. He was always of abbreviated height but grew steadily in length and breadth, and was quaint in appearance. One ear hung constantly down while the other was always cocked up. He had a fine, fluffy, mouse-coloured coat which cost him his life. One of the convicts who made ladies' shoes cast greedy eyes upon Kultiapka, and having felt his skin lured him into a corner, killed and flayed him. A little later the young wife of one of the officers appeared in a smart pair of velvet boots trimmed with mouse coloured fur.

Tanning and skin dressing was a trade much followed in the prison. Dogs which had been stolen by servants were brought in and sold. On one occasion a fine black dog of good breed was disposed of by a scamp of a footman for thirty kopecks. The poor beast must have anticipated what was in store for him, for he looked up at the convicts in a distressed, beseeching way, but could find no pity, and he was speedily hanged. The same fate overtook the prison goat, a beautiful white kid of whom every one was fond. The pretty creature was full of grace and was very playful, jumping on and off the kitchen table, wrestling with the convicts and always full of fun and spirits. He grew up into a fine, fat beast with magnificent horns, which it was proposed to gild and which were often decorated with flowers. It was the custom for the goat to march at the head of the convicts when returning from labour, and when the eyes of the choleric major fell upon it in the procession, he forthwith ordered it to be executed. The goat was killed and flayed; both carcass and skin were sold in the prison; the latter went to the leather dresser, the former, which fetched a ruble and fifty kopecks, was roasted and the flesh retailed among the convicts.

Other strange pets were a flock of geese, which somehow had been hatched within the enclosure, and as they grew up they attached themselves to the prisoners and would march out with them regularly to labour. When the drum beat and the parties assembled at the great gate, the geese came cackling, flapping their wings and hopping along. While the convicts worked, the geese pecked about close at hand until the time came for return, when they again joined the procession and marched with their friends solemnly back to the barracks, to the great amusement of the bystanders. The close attachment between the birds and their friends did not save the geese from having their necks twisted and being added to the dinner on a feast day.

The captive eagle did not take kindly to detention. It had been brought in wounded, with a broken wing and half dead. Nothing could domesticate or tame it. It gazed fiercely and fearlessly on the curious crowd and opened its beak as if determined to sell its life dearly. As soon as a chance came it hopped away on one leg, flapping its one uninjured wing, and hid in a far-off, inaccessible corner, from which it never emerged. The convicts often gathered to stare at it and would bait it with the dog Bull, who hesitated, in wholesome dread of the savage bird's beak and claws. The eagle long refused food, and although he finally took meat and drank water left with him, he would consume nothing that was given him by hand or when any one's eye was upon him. When no one was near, he would creep out of his corner and take a walk of a dozen steps, hopping and limping backward and forward with great regularity under the lee of the stockade. He resisted pugnaciously all overtures to friendship, and would suffer no one to pet him or pat him but pined away, lonely and irreconcilable, waiting only for death.

At last the convicts were moved to compassion for the caged bird, deprived of liberty like themselves. It was seriously discussed whether he ought not to be set free. So he was securely tied, taken out to the ramparts when the parties went to labour, and thrown out on the bare, barren steppe. The bird immediately hurried away, flapping his wounded wing and striving desperately to get out of sight of his captors. They looked after him enviously; they had given him the freedom they did not possess, a boon they hungered for unceasingly night and day, winter and summer, but especially when the sun shone bright and they could see the boundless plain stretching away in the blue distance beyond the river Irtysh and across the free Kirghiz Steppe.

Dostoyevski feelingly records his sensations when the day for his release at length arrived. The night before, as darkness fell, he went round the enclosure for the last time, revisiting every spot where he had suffered the bitter pangs of imprisonment, solitary and despairing,—the place where he had counted over and over again the thousands and thousands of days he had still to remain inside. The next morning, before the exodus for labour, he made the rounds to bid his comrades farewell; and many a coarse, horny hand was held out to him with hearty good-will. The generous souls gave him Godspeed, but others who were more envious turned their backs on him and would not reply to his kindly greetings. His last visit was to the blacksmith's shop. He went without escort, and placed his feet on the anvil, each in turn; the rivets were struck out of the basils and he was freed from his chains.

"Liberty! New life, resurrection from the dead! Unspeakable moment!"

CHAPTER VI
TIUMEN AND TOMSK

New route taken by exiles since opening of the Trans-Siberian railway—Increased numbers produced overcrowding in all prisons both in Europe and Asia—The "forwarding prisons" the cause of much distress—The Tiumen prison; cells, kitchen, hospital—Infectious diseases—Death-rate—Tomsk forwarding prison—Conditions worse than at Tiumen—The balagan or family "kamera"—Futile attempts to dispute incontrovertible evidence—"Étapes" or road prisons and "polu étapes" or half-way houses—Distance covered daily by the marching parties—The "telyegas" or country carts which carried the sick—Method of buying provisions from villagers en route—The "étape" of Achinsk—Infectious diseases in these prisons—The reports of Governor-General Anuchin—Sympathy of the Czar Alexander III.

The old order changeth slowly, and the hideous memories of the black and baleful past will long survive. The pages which record the disgraceful facts may be torn out of Russian prison history but they can never be eradicated or forgotten. Let it be granted that reforms and improvements have been introduced, and that some of the most glaring evils have been removed, we may doubt whether in the present condition of the empire, still shaken to its very base by disaster and disaffection, the betterment goes below the surface or will be lasting. The governing authorities in these troublous times have but little leisure to discuss penology, and although long since aroused to a lively sense of the shortcomings of their prison system, they are slow to mend their ways. Changes and ameliorations promised still tarry by the way, and there is but little hope that the frightful conditions so long prevailing have even in part disappeared.

The chief blot upon the method of transportation no longer exists, it is true. The wearisome, almost interminable march has been replaced by the long railway journey over the Trans-Siberian line, completed in 1897 and opened the following year for the conveyance of exiles. The convicts no longer spend a couple of years or more on a journey now performed in eight or ten days. Their sufferings are no longer protracted indefinitely, but for a brief space they are still locked up like cattle in dirty, ill-ventilated vans, and are still collected in the foul "forwarding prisons," whence they pass on for distribution to Eastern Siberia, the convict colony of Saghalien, or the outer darkness near the North Pole. A few well-planned and commodious new prisons have been erected in recent years, for which credit must be given to the prison administration, but they have applied only a partial remedy to existing conditions.

The exile route to-day naturally follows the new line of railway. From Moscow the road strikes south to Samara on the Volga, to which point a large passenger traffic is brought by the great water-way to board the trains. From Samara to Ufa on the west slope the Ural Mountains, and after scaling them the line descends to Chelyabinsk on the Siberian frontier. Here the convict travellers are divided into parties according to their destination. Some go north toward Tiumen and Tobolsk, others travel due east in the direction of Lake Baikal, and others start south for Semipalatinsk and the Altai.

The route before the railway was built was from Moscow, the centre of the home prison system, thence by train to Nizhni-Novgorod, and on by boat down the Volga through Kazan to Perm, and thence by train across the Ural Mountains to Ekaterinburg and Tiumen. All exiles of whatever class, without distinction or separation, travelled this way, and all halted at Tiumen, where they were made up into parties and forwarded to their several destinations.

Overcrowding was the curse of all Russian prisons; the cause of discomforts innumerable, inflicting untold suffering, producing deadly endemic and epidemic diseases. That it was the same everywhere, we are told on incontestable authority, and the futile attempts made by superficial inquirers to vindicate the government which is responsible are contemptible. To begin with St. Petersburg, the official report of the society for prisons stated that in 1880 the show prison, the Litovski Zamok, although built for seven hundred inmates, uniformly contained from nine hundred to a thousand; and the depot prison, supposed to hold two hundred, was always filled with double the number. The first named had 103 rooms nominally for eight hundred persons. These rooms, as described by an eye-witness, were exceedingly dirty, and he further says: "The 'black holes' are dreadful; they are absolutely deprived of light; a dark labyrinth leads to them and within all is wet, with rotten floors and dripping walls. A man coming from the outer air staggers away half asphyxiated. Specialists say that the healthiest man will surely die if he is kept there for three or four weeks. After a short stay prisoners went out exhausted; several could hardly stand on their feet."

As to the specific charge of overcrowding, a few details must carry conviction. The prison at Nizhni-Novgorod was built for three hundred, and generally held seven or eight hundred persons. In Poland there were four prisons occupying the space required for one. The prison at Perm was built in 1872 for 120 inmates, but in the same year it held just double that number and the cubical air space allotted to each individual was from 202 to 260 cubic feet, or, as Kropotkin puts it, it was just as if a man was living in a coffin eight feet by six feet. Another authority, the *Journal of Legal Medicine*, issued by the medical department of the Ministry of the Interior, gives the cubical contents as no more than 124 cubic feet per head. At Tomsk the prison was disgracefully overcrowded. It was built for nine hundred but contained over two thousand souls. At Samara the average prison population was 1,147, but the aggregate cubic capacity of all the prisons in the town was for 552 inmates. At Verkhni Udinsk an *ostrog* built for 140 prisoners was often packed with five hundred and even eight hundred inmates. On the whole, summing up the dreadful facts, an apologist of the Russian government admits that the prisons contain half as many more than the number originally intended.

Let us pass to the direct evidence of a perfectly veracious witness, speaking out of his own experience. George Kennan approached his self-imposed task with a judicial, well-balanced mind, quite unprejudiced against the Russian system, predisposed, if anything, to view it with favour. He paid a lengthy visit to the Tiumen forwarding prison, with the full permission of the authorities, who withheld nothing from his observation, premising only that it was greatly overcrowded and in a bad sanitary condition.

As to the first point, the figures were conclusive. It was a well-known fact that the prison was built originally for 550 inmates but was subsequently enlarged by the addition of detached barracks so as to hold nominally 850 prisoners. On the day Kennan visited it, the number was 1,741, as witnessed by a blackboard hanging up at the office door. In the first room entered, a *kamera* or cell, 35 feet long, 25 feet wide and 12 feet high, the accommodation and air space at the outside was for forty persons. On the night before, 160 had slept or, more exactly, passed the night in the room. The same dreadful superfluity of human beings existed throughout the entire prison.

"I looked around the cell," says Kennan. "There was practically no ventilation whatever, and the air was so poisoned and foul that I could hardly force myself to breathe it. We visited successively in the yard six *kameras* or cells, essentially like the first, and found in every one of them three or four times the number of prisoners for which it was intended, and five or six times the number for which it had adequate air space. In most of the cells there was not room enough on the sleeping platforms for all of the convicts, and scores of men slept every night on the foul, muddy floors, under the *nary*, 'sleeping platforms,' and in the gangways between them and the walls."

The main building, containing the kitchen, the workshops, the hospital and a large number of *kameras*, was in a worse sanitary condition than the barracks. The air in the corridors and cells, particularly on the second story, was indescribably foul. The oxygen had been breathed again and again; it was laden with fever germs from the unventilated hospital wards, fetid odours from diseased human lungs and unclean human bodies, and the stench of unmentionable receptacles. "It was like trying to breathe in an underground hospital drain," says Kennan. The kitchen was a dark, dirty room in the basement where three or four half naked cooks were baking large loaves and preparing soup. The bread was sour and heavy, but as good as that usually eaten by Russian peasants; the soup was found to be good and nutritious.

The hospital was on the third floor and the wards were larger and lighter than the *kameras*, but wholly unventilated; no disinfectants were in use, and the air was polluted to the last degree. The prospect of regaining health in such unwholesome dens was small. A man in robust condition must certainly become infected in a few weeks, and there was little hope for the recovery of the sick. All the worst disorders were to be found among the patients; scurvy, typhus fever, typhoid fever, acute bronchitis, rheumatism and syphilis. Only the patients affected by malignant typhus were isolated in a single ward. The women were separated from the men, but that was all. "The patients, both men and women, seemed to be not only desperately sick, but hopeless and heart broken." The mortality was excessive. Typhus was epidemic every year. The prison was uniformly overcrowded; it had been built for eight hundred and generally contained eighteen hundred. Some scanty ventilation was possible when the windows could be opened, but in the stormy autumn or bitter winter no fresh air could be admitted.

According to the official reports of the inspectors of exile transportation, in the eleven years between 1876 and 1886 the greatest number of deaths in the Tiumen prison hospital was 354, the lowest 175, the average 270. This is an unparalleled death-rate. In various European prisons the rate is on the average as follows:—England, 1.4 per cent.; France, 3.8 per cent.; Austria, 3.5 per cent.; Belgium, 1.8 per cent.; United States, 1.7 per cent. "In the Tiumen forwarding prison it was 29.5 per cent., or almost 300 per thousand.... This would entirely annihilate a fixed population in from two and a half to four years,"—a death-rate such as this, in the words of Mr. Cable, "exceeds that of any pestilence that ever fell on Europe in the Middle Ages."

The female prison was in a separate yard within a high stockade of sharpened logs. The *kameras* were clean and well-lighted; floors and sleeping platforms had been scrubbed; the rooms were not so densely overcrowded, and the air was purer than on the men's side. But the condition of the third detached prison, that for exiled families, in which men, women and children were herded together to the number of three hundred, was horrible. It was overcrowded; the air was heavy and foul; "dozens of children were crying from hunger and wretchedness; and the men and women looked tired, sleepless and dejected." All the women were voluntarily accompanying their husbands or fathers into banishment.

The disgraceful state of the Tiumen forwarding prison was perfectly well known to the authorities, and has been strongly commented upon in official reports. How far amendment has proceeded I have no definite information, although we may hope that the diversion of the outward stream of exiles since the opening of the Trans-Siberian railway has greatly reduced the excessive demands upon the imperfect accommodation. But there is another forwarding prison further eastward and at one time on the direct line of exile traffic. This is at the city of Tomsk, which is actually fifty miles distant from the railway, because the local authorities refused to pay the blackmail demanded by the projectors of the line to bring it through, or within easy reach of the city. Before railway days, the convicts travelled in barges on the river Tobol from Tiumen to Tomsk. These barges were planned to accommodate six hundred on each voyage; they were towed by steamers and made the journey in from seven to ten days, completing eighteen trips during the season of open navigation, and thus they transported annually between ten thousand and eleven thousand souls.

If the Tiumen prison was in horrible condition, that of Tomsk was infinitely worse. Its deplorable state was frankly admitted to George Kennan by the authorities when they granted him permission to visit it. "I think you will find it the worst prison in Siberia," said the acting governor of the province of Tomsk. What else was to be expected when the buildings were filled with more than twice the number of inmates which they could properly accommodate? The Tomsk forwarding prison was designed to hold fourteen hundred, but three thousand or even four thousand were habitually crammed into it. The numbers arriving exceeded the power of distribution, and week by week a residuum remained to increase the permanent population. The *étapes*, or halting stations along the road, could accommodate only a limited number and there were not enough troops to provide for more than one marching party each week.

The Tomsk forwarding prison is described by Mr. Kennan, who saw it in 1885, as, "a stockaded camp or enclosure three acres in extent, lying on open ground outside the city." Within were some fifteen to twenty log buildings grouped about a pyramidal church tower. Each wooden building in the enclosure was a one-storied barrack prison of square logs with board roofs, heavily grated windows and massive iron doors secured with padlocks. There were eight of these, each constituting a prison ward and each divided into two *kameras*, one on each side of a central corridor running through the building. Each ward or building was calculated to hold 190 inmates, but was crowded with at least three hundred. Each cell was about forty feet square and the air space was seven-eighths of a cubic fathom per head. The cells were fairly well lighted, but the atmosphere was pestilential and the temperature from the natural heat of the prisoners' bodies was fifteen or twenty degrees higher than the external air. The usual sleeping platforms ran across the cells, but there was not room on them for half of the number confined there, and the other half was forced to sleep beneath the platforms, or on the floor in the adjoining gangways. These lay there on the mud-stained and filthy floor, without pillows, blankets or bedclothing. They were in such a grievous state that they complained feelingly of the heat, foulness and oppressiveness of the air and declared that it was impossible to move about in the day time or to get rest at night.

The same evils were present in every cell. But the horrors culminated in the "family" room or *balagan*, the long, low shed of rough pine boards,—a frame work hastily put together and with sides of thin white cotton sheeting. There were three of these crammed full of family parties, men, women and children. The shed was surrounded by a foul ditch half full of filth which soaked through and from under the cotton-sheeting wall. The only light that penetrated within the windowless *balagan* was through this wall of cotton. The place was packed with hundreds of occupants,—"weary-eyed men, haggard women and ailing children," sitting and lounging about the sleeping platforms and on the broken boards of the floor through which exuded all kinds of abominations. The air was insufferably fetid from the great numbers of infants unwashed and wholly uncared for. Wet underclothing, washed in the camp kettles, was hanging from the beams to dry; an indistinguishable chaos of bags, bundles and domestic utensils encumbered the floor, and the crowd was so closely packed that people could not move without touching each other. No remedy, no alleviation was possible. The cold at night in these cotton enclosed walls, or the damp heat and imperfect ventilation in the bath-house—which many would have preferred—were equally fatal to infant life. Detention in these wretched apologies for shelters was greatly prolonged. No change of clothing was provided; a man wore the same shirt for months, until it almost dropped off, in dirty ragged scraps, full of vermin. Not strangely was it thought a welcome relief when the orders came to take the road. The toilsome march with its incessant hardships and exhausting fatigue was preferable to the fixed residence in a forwarding prison.

The hospital at Tomsk was in some respects better than that at Tiumen; it occupied a separate building, and was kept in better order. There were always more patients than beds to receive them, and the surplus in various stages of acute disease lay about on benches or on the floor. Despite the overcrowding, the place was kept fairly clean, the bed clothing was fresh and plentiful and the air was less polluted than at Tiumen. The percentage of the sick varied according to the season. It rose in November, when the population was at its highest, to twenty-five per cent., and among the diseases malignant typhus, the true type of the ancient, but now happily rare, "gaol fever," was always largely present. There were twenty-four hundred cases of illness in the year and at the most crowded time there have been 450 cases in the hospital with beds for only 150 patients.

The prison surgeon, one of the most humane and devoted of his class, Dr. Orzheshko, has described his experience covering fifteen years. In November, he says, "three hundred men and women dangerously sick lay on the floor in rows, most of them without pillows or bed clothing; and in order to find even floor space for them we had to put them so close together that I could not walk between them, and a patient could not cough or vomit without coughing or vomiting into his own face or into the face of the man lying beside him. The atmosphere in the wards became so terribly polluted that I fainted repeatedly upon coming into the hospital in the morning, and my assistants had to revive me by dashing water into my face. In order to change or purify the air, we were forced to keep the windows open; and as winter set in, this so chilled the rooms, that we could not maintain ... a temperature higher than five or six degrees Réamur above the freezing point."

This hospital was so saturated with contagious disease that it stood condemned, and deserved to be burned down. Official procrastination delayed its destruction, but in 1887 a sum of 30,000 rubles was granted for the erection of a new hospital, which is, presumably, now occupied. It was high time to make a change. The city of Tomsk, the capital of Siberia, the great centre of Siberian trade, flourishing, prosperous and increasing, naturally became alarmed. The free inhabitants were threatened with the spread of dire epidemic diseases. The local press, defying the censorship, eloquently denounced the horrible condition due to the vast accumulation of excessive numbers in the forwarding prison, and the resultant evils in sickness and mortality. The newspapers stated incontrovertible facts. The death-rate in the city of Tomsk was fifty per thousand per annum, sufficiently large, but in the prison it was three hundred per thousand. Typhus was the predominating disease, accompanied by smallpox, diphtheria, measles and scarlatina. This typhus constituted 56.4 per cent. of all the sickness in the forwarding prison in 1886, 62.6 per cent. in 1887 and 23 per cent. in 1888. The corresponding death-rate in these years was 23.2, 21 and 13.1 per cent.

A violent controversy was aroused between the enterprising and outspoken American investigator, Mr. George Kennan, and a well-known English explorer, Mr. H. de Windt, who undertook to contest the statements, and, indeed, to deny the facts set forth by Mr. Kennan, plainly condemning them as the phantasy of a disordered imagination and boldly affirming that such a place as the Tomsk forwarding prison "does not exist." Mr. de Windt's arguments are based upon the negative evidence of his own experience. He declares that he saw nothing of the horrors described, but then he never saw or closely inspected the prisons incriminated. He was, no doubt, admitted to certain prisons, which he visited under the auspices of the authorities, and he reported upon them hastily and on imperfect knowledge. Mr. Kennan's painful story is so completely sustained by Russian official reports and the open condemnation of the Siberian press, that it is entitled to full credence and may be relied upon as absolutely trustworthy and conclusive. His account of Tiumen and Tomsk must take a prominent place in the history of penal institutions.

The exile system called the *étapes* or "road prisons" into being. They were very numerous and were planted at intervals of every twenty-five or forty miles, and as this distance was beyond the limit of a single day's march, half-way houses, or *polu étapes*, were to be met with regularly along the road. Each *étape* was the headquarters of a detachment of soldiers who formed the convoy or escort of the convicts moving eastward. At the *polu étapes* there were no troops. The head of each convoy was a commissioned officer styled the *nachalnik*.

The marching parties covered 330 miles every month, doing from fifteen to twenty miles on two succeeding days and resting on the third. Thus a party leaving Tomsk on Monday morning reached a *polu étape* that night, slept there and passed on to another regular *étape* on Wednesday, where they halted for twenty-four hours. On Thursday the journey was resumed with a fresh escort, a *polu étape* was reached that night, and a regular *étape* the next, and so on, day after day and week after week for many months. Until 1883, there was no separation of the sexes on the march, but after that date single men were excluded from the family parties in which women and children were included. Terrible demoralisation was previously the rule in the constantly overcrowded *étapes*, and the grossest offences were commonly committed.

The departure of a marching party from the forwarding prison was generally fixed at eight o'clock in the morning, when the *telyegas*, or country carts, for the conveyance of the sick and infirm, began to collect in front of the prison gate. Next appeared the prison blacksmith with his anvil and portable forge, to test the fetters as the convicts came forth, and after he had satisfied himself that the rivets were fast and the basils had not been bent, an under officer doled out ten kopecks to each individual, and the convicts were formed in line, by classes, for convenience of inspection and calling the roll. The hard-labour convicts removed their gray visorless caps to show that their crowns were half shaved according to regulation. From the other sides of their heads hung a mat of long, coarse and dishevelled hair. At length the whole party, numbering from three to four hundred, assembled in the street; each convict carried a gray linen two-bushel bag for the storage of his personal effects. Many possessed tea-kettles, dangling from the waist belts that supported the leg irons, and one or two might be seen with a favourite dog in their arms. All the men were dressed alike in long gray overcoats over coarse linen shirts and loose gray trousers. The women wore no distinctive uniform, but were dressed mostly in peasant costume with gaily coloured handkerchiefs on their

CHAPTER VII
VAGABONDAGE AND UNIONS

Peculiar phases of criminality to be found in Siberian prisons—Country overrun with convict fugitives—Terrible privations suffered by these vagrants—The "call of the cuckoo"—The vagrants known as "brodyagi"—Number of runaway convicts in the summer months said to exceed thirty thousand—The formation of the "artel" or union in all companies of convicts—The power and methods of the "Ivans" or recidivists in the "artel"—Leo Deutsch's story—Life of the politicals in the Middle Kara state prison—The "Sirius" or student who worked during the night—The humane governor, Colonel Kanonovich—He resigns rather than obey the government's orders that the prisoners should be perpetually chained to wheelbarrows.

Certain types of criminals and some peculiar phases of criminality have grown up in Russian, and especially in Siberian prisons. They are mainly due to the negation of proper penitentiary principles and the absence of any fixed methods of treatment. Callous indifference has generally alternated with brutal repression and savage, disciplinary punishments. The chief result has been the growth of classes of criminals seldom seen elsewhere. The so-called "habitual offender" is to be met with strongly developed and in a peculiarly vicious form in Siberia. The whole country is overrun with fugitive convicts who have made good their escape in various fashions. Some have run from the marching parties, carrying their lives in their hands as they braved the bullets of the generally straight-shooting soldiers of the escort; others have successfully evaded the police at remote points of settlement as established exiles; not a few have benefited by the exchange of identity with some one who remained behind. All have become wild men of the woods, the terror of all peaceable members of society whom they may come across in the scattered settlements or single houses of the sparsely inhabited districts. Many thousands of these vagrants are at large in the summer months, when they may live in the open air and subsist as best they can on what they find or steal. Large numbers are recaptured; many perish from cold and starvation when winter approaches; many more give themselves up voluntarily to save their lives, accepting the severest flogging or a new sentence as the penalty of their escape.

Yet they are incorrigible wanderers and pass their lives in short periods of freedom and longer doses of confinement. When Kennan saw a marching party start, he was shown convicts who were treading the dolorous road for the sixth time. The captain of the escort assured him that he had known cases in which the journey had been repeated sixteen times. In other words, the vagrant had crossed Siberia just thirty-two times on foot, and had, therefore, walked as much as if he had twice made the circuit of the globe at the Equator.

The passionate craving for freedom has been well described by Dostoyevski. "At the first song of the lark throughout all Siberia and Russia, men set out on the tramp; God's creatures, if they can break their prison and escape into the woods.... They go vagabondising where they please, wherever life seems to them most agreeable and easy; they drink and eat what they can find; at night they sleep undisturbed and without a care in the woods or in a field;... saying good night only to the stars; and the eye that watches them is the eye of God. It is not altogether a rosy lot: sometimes they suffer hunger and fatigue 'in the service of General Cuckoo.' Often enough the wanderers have not a morsel of bread to keep their teeth going for days at a time.... They are almost all brigands and thieves by necessity rather than inclination.... This life in the woods, wretched and fearful as it is, but still free and adventurous, has a mysterious seduction for those who have experienced it."

A curious illustration of this consuming passion is to be found in the case of an aged convict who had become the servant of a high official at the Kara gold mines. This man ran away periodically at the return of spring, and although suffering always the same terrible privations, was brought back in irons. At last, at the fateful moment, he came to his master and begged that he might be locked up. "I am a *brodyaga*, heart and soul, quite irreclaimable, and I cannot resist the cuckoo's call. Please do me the favour to put me under lock and key so that I cannot go off." He was closely confined until the summer passed, and when the fever of unrest left him, he was released and became quiet, contented and docile as ever. A convict who has earned conditional freedom and received a grant of land, may have married, had children and lived quietly for some years, when suddenly some day he will have disappeared, abandoning wife and family, to the stupefaction of everybody. Vagrancy is in his blood. He probably was a deserter before his conviction; the passion for wandering has always possessed him. He has hungered after a change of lot, and nothing would hold him, not even his family, much less police surveillance or prison bars.

The largest number of these vagabonds, or "passportless" men, as they are called, have begun at the earliest opportunity to make a break for liberty while on the road between the *étapes*. As the party was being marshalled after the midday rest, or when it reached some defile or stretch of broken ground, a simultaneous dash was made by several through the marching cordon of guards. Fire was then opened instantaneously, and one or more of the fugitives fell while the rest got away. If the rush was made near some wood and cover could be gained, the escape was successful. The first step on reaching a safe shelter was to remove the leg irons by pounding the basils into an oblong shape with a stone. Then the fugitive's face was turned a term of imprisonment, after which he could count upon release as an ordinary exile.

This is no fanciful story. Cases were of constant occurrence. Leo Deutsch, when on his way to the Kara mines, was seriously approached by a comrade on the march, who suggested an exchange and showed unblushingly how it might be carried out. This man was a veteran "Ivan," a criminal aristocrat and dandy among his fellows; he wore a white shirt with a gay tie under his gray overcoat, and a brightly coloured scarf round his waist, to which his chains were cleverly attached so that they did not rattle or incommode him when walking. The suggestion was nothing less than a cold-blooded murder. The substitute to be provided was to have some personal resemblance to Deutsch, and would take his place with the other politicals one day, and disappear the next. When his body should be picked up presently in a neighbouring stream, it would be supposed that Deutsch had committed suicide, while in reality, still alive and hearty, he was to be disguised as the substitute who had been permanently "removed" to make a place for him. The price of this atrocity was a few rubles, twenty or thirty at most, and the blood money was to be divided among the murderers, with a large contribution to the revenues of the union.

It was to the interest of the *artel* to encourage these exchanges and insist upon their punctual performance. The substitute was never permitted to back out of his bargain. He generally belonged to the class contemptuously styled "biscuits," and the name suited these pale, emaciated creatures, the pariahs of the party, upon whom fell all the dirty, disagreeable jobs. These poor wretches had lost all power of will, and cared for nothing but the cards that had been their ruin. They stole all they could lay their hands on, except from the "Ivans," who would have retaliated with a murderous thrashing, justified on the ground that the thief had stolen from his own people. The condition of these "biscuits" was heart-rending, especially in bad weather, when, clothed in rags that barely covered their nakedness, they ran rather than walked on the line of march so as to keep themselves warm. Their only pleasure was in gambling, when anything and everything was staked, even the government clothing for which they were responsible and for losing which they were punished cruelly.

Next in importance to the chief, the storekeeper was a prominent official in the union. He had bought his place, bidding the highest price for it when put up at auction, and he had acquired the exclusive right to sell provisions to the prisoners, and to supply them secretly with tobacco, spirits and playing cards. The last mentioned were in constant use and the games were eagerly watched. When a winner was lucky, it was customary for him to stand treat to his starving comrades. The storekeeper also, on the expiration of his office, would entertain everyone with a feast when the prisoners would hungrily eat their fill, crying, "It is the storekeeper who pays."

There is now, however, little chance of any such extended organisation among the convicts on the journey or in the forwarding prisons. The officials have learned how to prevent and break up such combinations and more recent regulations have rendered them inoperative. So the old *brodyagi* must lament for the good old days and the power that they once exercised.

Some curious details of the organisation of the *artel* in the Middle Kara, or state prison for politicals, are given by Leo Deutsch. It was formed for domestic administration and was worked fairly and equitably for the general good. Coöperation was the leading principle. All issues of food, the daily rations for the whole number, were collected and afterward divided with such additions as were provided out of a common fund obtained by general contribution of moneys received by prisoners from their friends at home. This fund was expended in three ways: one part went to the "stock pot" as explained above, to supplement the food; a second was applied to help prisoners about to be released; and the third was divided as pocket money among the whole number, to be spent according to individual taste, in buying small luxuries or books approved by the authorities. The *starosta* kept strict account; no actual money passed hands; paper orders circulated and were debited to each member on a monthly balance sheet, with the result brought out as "plus" or "minus." It was the same as in ordinary life; some thriftless people were always in debt; the impecunious hoped to get clear at Christmas time when gifts came in, but if still on the wrong side, the "minus" was "whitewashed" by the consent of the *artel* but not always with the concurrence of the debtor, who was sometimes too proud to accept the favour.

Under this union, life in common was admirably organised, with a division of labour and a regular roster of employment. Work was of two classes; for private purposes, and for the general good. The former included washing of clothes and mending, the latter cooking, cleaning, attending to the steam bath and the various domestic services. No pains were spared to insure cleanliness. All rooms occupied by the prisoners were scrupulously washed and kept tidy; the bed-boards and floors were regularly scrubbed with hot water; the beds were aired; tables and benches were washed in the yard; all sanitary appliances were thoroughly disinfected. Proper ventilation was insisted upon, and close attention was paid to hygienic conditions. All worked cheerfully, and illness only was allowed as an exemption. The cooking was done by groups of five each which served for a week at a time. A head cook, an assistant cook for invalids, and two helpers made up the group. This was hard work, fatiguing while it lasted, but a relief to the monotonous life. The kitchen became a sort of club-house, where men came to laugh and jest and play practical jokes, a imposed an impossible duty on me, and I cannot perform it and keep an approving conscience."

Colonel Kanonovich fortunately had many influential friends, and the accusations brought against him could not injure him permanently. He was an officer of the Cossacks and was appointed to another command in the Trans-Baikal, and later promoted to be a general officer, in charge of the enlarged penal colony of Saghalien. He also supervised the erection of the new Verkhni Udinsk prison, in which a praiseworthy and conspicuous effort at reform was subsequently made. The building of the political prison at Middle Kara was under his direction, but he left just before it was occupied and was in no wise responsible for the atrocities committed there.

CHAPTER VIII
TREATMENT OF POLITICALS

Withdrawal of privileges accorded to politicals—Lunatics confined in association with other prisoners—Suicides—Many escapes attempted—Fresh deprivations—The politicals separated and confined in common prisons of the Kara district—Subjected to "dungeon conditions"—Much disease—Finally transferred to the state prison—Hunger strike which lasted thirteen days—Some remarkable female revolutionists—A hunger strike instituted by the women—Attempts to pacify them—The resignation of the governor Masyukov demanded—Madame Sigida strikes Masyukov in the face—Subjected to flogging and dies—Three of her companions commit suicide—Thirteen of the men determine to put an end to their lives—Governors, good and bad—Deutsch's account of Nikolin's régime—The atrocities committed by the governor Patrin at Saghalien.

The changed attitude of the government toward the state prisoners at Kara dated, as we have said, from the end of the year 1880, under the initiative of Loris Melikov, and this action, so inconsistent with his supposed views as a liberal minister, has never been explained. Kennan suggests that it was caused by bad advice, carelessly adopted. But, as Leo Deutsch tells us, the harsh régime was introduced at a time when the revolutionary agitation had revived in great strength, and the dominant bureaucracy was more than ever on the defensive, ready to wreak its revengeful feelings upon the captives it held in durance. In any case, the orders issued evidenced a retrograde policy and a revival of the old methods of repression with new punishments superadded. All existing privileges, even the most trivial, were withdrawn. A peremptory stop was put to all correspondence with relatives and friends; work in the open air for ordinary criminal convicts was forbidden; and all the politicals who had finished their sentences of imprisonment and were living in the "free command" were again immured, with the old inflictions of leg irons and half shaved heads. At three days' notice they were sent back to prison, many of them leaving their wives and children alone and unprotected in a vicious and disorderly penal settlement.

When they reëntered they were herded with the rest in the new political prison at or near the Kara Lower Diggings, a building somewhat better than those for common criminals, being larger, more spacious and better lighted, with four *kameras*, each warmed with a brick oven and provided with the conventional *nary* or sleeping platforms. At first the windows looked out upon the valley, an open if not very picturesque prospect. This was the case in other prisons for all criminal convicts, but it did not please Governor-General Anuchin, who ordered the whole place to be shut in by a high stockade. "A prison is not a palace," he cynically declared, as he condemned his fellow creatures to be deprived of all view and restricted in the matter of light. Anuchin, in his report to the Czar, dated two years later, admits that the life of state criminals was "unbearable," but quite forgot how far he himself contributed to their sufferings.

Under the brutal system in force, insane companions, often raging lunatics, were confined with the rest. There were no asylums in Siberia, and the insane lived in association with the sane, adding much to the miseries of both. "In more than one place in the Trans-Baikal we were startled," says Kennan, "as we entered a crowded prison *kamera*, by some uncared-for lunatic, who sprang suddenly toward us with a wild cry or with a burst of hysterical laughter.... It is easier and cheaper to make the prison comrades of a lunatic take care of him than to keep him in seclusion and provide him with an attendant. For educated political prisoners, who dread insanity more than anything else, it is, of course, terribly depressing to have constantly before them, in the form of a wrecked intelligence, an illustration of the possible end of their own existence."

Several painful episodes soon followed the recommittal of the "free command" to prison. One was the suicide of Eugene Semyanovski, a young journalist connected with the underground journal *Onward*, who had gained his conditional freedom and lost it. He left a letter to his father bemoaning his hard fate, written the night before his reëntry to prison, and shot himself in his bed. Another political hanged himself in the prison bath-house, and a third poisoned himself by drinking water in which he had soaked lucifer matches. Another most affecting incident was the mental failure of Madame Kovalevskaya, a brilliant woman, who had been actively concerned in the revolutionary propaganda as the only means of securing free institutions in the empire. She was sentenced to penal servitude at Kara, where she presently joined the "free command." Her husband was also exiled, but was sent to Minusinsk in Eastern Siberia, so that no less than a thousand miles intervened between the pair. Their only child had been left behind at Kiev in Russia. Madame Kovalevskaya's insanity declared itself after she went back to Kara prison and while Colonel Kanonovich was still in command, and she was then allowed to join her husband, but after partial recovery she was returned to Kara. Eventually, after the cowardly oppression of her comrades, she committed suicide.

Another consequence of the increased severity in the treatment of politicals was their widespread determination to break prison. Many escapes were attempted, and although they were for the most part frustrated, the feeling of unrest was so general that the authorities resolved to use more severe methods of coercion. A high official stated that they meant "to reduce the prison to order and give the politicals a lesson." Daily life was made more and more irksome; privileges, great and small, were withdrawn; all books were removed; money, underclothing, beds and bedding were taken from them; they might possess nothing more than the bare necessaries allowed to ordinary convicts. But worse than all, the whole number, kept hitherto in one prison, was broken up into small parties and distributed among the various common prisons of the Kara district, where they were to be treated under "dungeon conditions." This treatment meant more than the deprivation of small luxuries as above mentioned; it also entailed the loss of all exercise in the open air or communication with the outside, and a diet of only black rye bread and water, with sometimes a little broth thickened with barley.

The removal was made forcibly. Cossacks were concentrated at the Lower Diggings in anticipation of resistance, or perhaps to provoke it, and suddenly a descent was made upon the prison in the dead of night. A strong, armed force marched into the prison with bayonets fixed, and seized the poor politicals as they were roused from sleep. They were stripped, searched, driven forth with blows and otherwise cruelly maltreated. The next morning, having been robbed and despoiled of all their private possessions, they were marched off under escorts to the other Kara prisons. They marched continuously for ten miles without food or drink, or a halt for rest, and one man who was chained to a wheelbarrow rolled it all the way. Goaded to desperation, those prisoners who were not ironed attacked the Cossacks with stones, but they were speedily overpowered. They arrived in a state of utter exhaustion at the common prisons, and were lodged two and two in "secret" cells, hitherto employed only for the safe custody of the worst criminals, which were bare rooms with no more furniture than the open *parasha*, or bucket, and with only the stone floor to sleep on.

These essentially "dungeon conditions" spent in the secret cells of the ordinary criminals were continued for two months, and at length the health of the politicals became grievously impaired. Foul air, insufficient food, close confinement and the lack of all exercise brought on an epidemic of scurvy, which resulted in serious illnesses in many cases. They were still without underclothing, bedding or nourishing food, although the authorities held prisoners' moneys out of which the cost might have been defrayed. All the politicals were then transferred to the Lower Diggings, and lodged in the new cells of the state prison. Seven or eight prisoners were crowded into a narrow space obtained by dividing each *kamera* into three parts by the creation of partitions. The sleeping platform nearly filled each interior and left little standing room, and the pollution of the air was "simply maddening." Protest and remonstrance were continuous, and only ceased when threats of flogging were made, a form of punishment never yet inflicted on politicals.

At length the unhappy victims of such savage repression had recourse to a "hunger strike," the last terrible weapon of the otherwise helpless prisoners. It is a strange and almost incomprehensible fact that the Russian prison authorities have always yielded to the pressure exercised by a number of prisoners resolutely determined to starve themselves to death. Our deepest sympathy must be accorded to the great courage that inspires this last appeal against intolerable cruelties. We admire and understand it, but are amazed that it should be so effectual with the brutal and otherwise insensible oppressors. When the much wronged politicals delivered their ultimatum, the authorities at first received it with indifference, but soon became anxious and at length despairing, as the refusal to take food was steadfastly persisted in. Not a morsel of sustenance was taken. "As day after day passed, the stillness of death gradually settled down upon the prison. The starving convicts, too weak and apathetic even to talk to one another, lay in rows, like dead men, upon the plank sleeping platforms, and the only sounds heard in the building were the footsteps of the sentries, and now and then the incoherent mutterings of the insane."

Overtures were made and amelioration in their condition was promised; fears of flogging were ridiculous, the officials said, and nothing of the kind had been contemplated. But the strike continued, for the strikers had no confidence in the plausible assurances of the governor. On the tenth day of starvation, the state of affairs was desperate. The indomitable sufferers had reached the last stage of physical exhaustion, and release by death seemed close at hand. The struggle was anxiously watched from St. Petersburg. Telegrams passed daily between the local authorities and the minister of the interior, who could only suggest medical intervention, which does not seem to have been tried beyond feeling pulses and taking the bodily temperatures. The wives of the strikers were finally granted the unusual privilege of an interview, on condition that they would implore their husbands to take food. These loving entreaties, backed by fresh promises from the commandant, finally overcame the resolution of the politicals, and on the thirteenth day of abstention the great hunger strike ended.

The physical endurance called forth by a hunger strike has been well described by Leo Deutsch, who was driven to refuse food by his ill-usage in the Odessa prison in the early stages of his sentence. His well-known character for sturdy defiance had so disturbed the prison authorities that they had taken extraordinary precautions to secure him, by lodging him in a dark underground cell, with no bedding except straw infested with rats, and no ventilation. He decided to starve himself in protest. They threatened to feed him artificially; he retorted that he knew how to bring on sickness. Then they listened to his very justifiable protest, and on the fourth day he ended his strike. He says, "It was only when I began to eat that I realised how fearfully hungry I was. I could have devoured an ox.... During the two following days I felt very seedy, as though I had had a bad illness."

Hunger strikes were more especially the weapon of the weaker sex, although there was no weakness among the women revolutionists, and the movement owed much of its vigour and vitality to their indomitable courage and unconquerable strength of character. In the days to come, when the great, patient people of a cruelly oppressed and misgoverned land have achieved its emancipation, ample justice must be done to the feminine champions, who entered boldly into the fray and fought strenuously for the vindication of the rights of their fellow countrymen to freedom and independence. Many of their names will then be honoured and revered with the greatest of those known to history. Russian women of all stations, and some of them of the highest rank, have won the admiration of the whole world, for their disregard of self, the sacrifice of all ease and comfort, and the braving of the worst dangers and the most poignant sufferings in their constant efforts to oppose political slavery. We may be inclined to quarrel with their methods, overlooking the greatness of their provocation, and believing that nothing could justify the violent means adopted, but we cannot withhold our sympathy for the ardent souls who have dared employ them.

Some of the most remarkable female revolutionists were concerned with the hunger strikes in Eastern Siberia and were victims of the methods inflicted in retaliation of outraged discipline. There were those who emulated the crime of Vera Zassulich, who in 1878 tried, but failed, to shoot General Trepov, the chief of the St. Petersburg police, for ordering the corporal punishment of a political prisoner. Madame Kutitonskaya fired at General Ilyashevich, the governor of the Trans-Baikal, to avenge the intolerable ill-usage of the political prisoners on the 11th of May, 1882. Madame Hope Sigida struck Colonel Masyukov in the face, to shame him into withdrawing from Kara, where he was commandant of the political prisons, and where his indignant female charges had boycotted him, insisting upon his removal. Madame Elizabeth Kovalskaya deliberately showed her contempt for the governor-general of the Amur, Baron Korv, by refusing to rise in his presence, and was in consequence removed to the central prison in Verkhni-Udinsk.

The lives and antecedents of some of these female exiles who suffered so bitterly for their opinions, merit special notice. Maria Kutitonskaya was a pupil in a girls' school at Odessa and joined the revolutionists while still a young girl. She was arrested with Lisogub, a wealthy man who lived in extreme poverty in order to devote his fortune to the revolutionary funds, and she was condemned to four years' hard labour. Madame Kutitonskaya was the uncompromising foe of the prison officials and constantly resisted the irksome rules imposed. With three other women, Mesdames Kovalevskaya, Bogomoletz and Elena Rossikova, she was removed to Irkutsk and there got into contest with the chief of the police, against whom they organised a hunger strike in which they persisted for ten or eleven days, until the prison doctor grew alarmed and representation was made to the governor of the district who brought the police officer to reason.

Madame Kutitonskaya was a lady of great personal attractions, with fair face and winning manner, and was greatly admired. After her attempt to assassinate General Ilyashevich, she was closely confined on bread and water in a damp, gloomy dungeon. The ordinary convicts brought her food, fell at her feet and christened her "Cupidon Skaya," as a pet name in recognition of her beauty. The story of her murderous attack is told in full by Kennan.

"Stirred to the very depths of her soul by a feeling of intense indignation" at the shameful ill-treatment of the politicals at Kara, she did not hesitate to sacrifice her life and that of her unborn child by committing a deed that must give publicity to the wrongs she and her companions had suffered. When interned in the town of Aksha in the Trans-Baikal district, she purchased a small revolver from a released criminal colonist, ran away from her place of banishment and made for Chita, where the governor resided. She was too pretty to travel alone without attracting attention and when she reached Chita she was arrested. At the police station she did not deny her identity but pleaded that she was eager to have an interview with the governor. Accordingly, she was detained in the reception room while a message was sent to Ilyashevich which brought the general to her. They had neglected to search her, and she held her revolver ready cocked under a handkerchief as the governor entered, shooting him forthwith through the lungs. The wound was not mortal, and the assailant was promptly seized and carried off to the Chita prison.

Her subsequent treatment was abominable. She was lodged in a "secret" cell, cold, dark, dirty, too short to allow her to lie down at full length, and too low to permit her to stand upright. Her own dress and underclothing were taken from her, contrary to the usual treatment of women politicals, and a ragged petticoat infested with vermin was given her in exchange. Despite her condition, she was obliged to lie for three months without bed-clothing on the bare floor. Serious illness seized her, and she begged at least for a little straw to sleep on; it was contemptuously denied her. But for the succour brought by her criminal comrades, she could not have survived until her trial. This at last took place before a court-martial, and she was sentenced to be hanged. Had she made known her pregnancy, it might have gained her a reprieve, but she forbore to speak, although she suffered bitterly at the prospect of becoming the murderess of her unborn child. The feeling was intensified by the dreadful thought that it might remain alive after she had died. The question was solved by the unexpected leniency of the government, by whom the death penalty was commuted to penal servitude for life at the creditable intercession of her intended victim. She was then removed in midwinter to Irkutsk, and would have been entirely unprovided with warm clothing but for the charity of her criminal comrades, who gave her felt boots and a sheepskin overcoat. The immediate result of her treatment was the birth of a still-born child, and she herself succumbed eventually to lung trouble.

Madame Kovalevskaya is described by Deutsch, who knew her well, as one of the most notable women in the revolutionary movement. She was the daughter of a landed proprietor named Vorontsov, her brother was Basil Vorontsov, a well known political economist, and she married Kovalevskaya, a tutor in a gymnasium of Kiev. She had thrown in her lot with the advanced party in the early sixties, and she devoted herself constantly to the work. In appearance she was short in stature, gipsy-like in appearance, alert and energetic in manner, keen witted, ready and logical in speech. She took the lead in theoretical discussions, imparting life and spirit into debate without becoming personal or hurting people's feelings. Her gifts were exceptional; she was a brilliant creature born to play a distinguished part in society. At an early age she had opened a peasant school and sought to improve the mental condition of the poorer classes. Her efforts soon drew upon her the attention of the police, and she was harried and thwarted by them until they drove her into the ranks of the revolutionary party. The circle in Kiev to which she belonged was broken up, its members were arrested and she and her husband were exiled to Siberia. Her fiery and uncompromising temper kept her in constant antagonism with the authorities, and her active protest against the ill-treatment of her comrade politicals brought her prominently to the front, with the fatal consequences already described.

Of her three friends, one, Madame Kutitonskaya, has been mentioned; a second was Sophia Bogomoletz, whose maiden name was Prisyetskaya, and who was the daughter of a rich landowner of Poltava. She had graduated at a medical school in St. Petersburg and, having married a doctor, threw herself ardently into revolutionary work. She was arrested as a member of the South Russian Workmen's Union and was sent to ten years' hard labour in Siberia with a companion, Madame Kovalskaya. They escaped from the Irkutsk prison but were recaptured in a few weeks, before they could leave the city. When brought back, the customary search was personally supervised by Colonel Soliviov, an adjutant of the governor-general and a man of vicious character, and by his order the two women were stripped naked before him. After this disgrace to humanity and the uniform he wore, he went immediately to one of the men's wards and boasted of the shameful deed, adding contemptuously, "Your political women are not much to look at." Whereupon one of those present, Shchedrin, who had been a school-teacher before sentence, struck the brute upon the mouth, calling him coward and liar. For this violent protest Shchedrin was condemned to be chained perpetually to a wheelbarrow as already described.

Madame Bogomoletz was punished with an additional five years' penal sentence, to be passed as a "probationer" prisoner, serving the full term without the remission granted to others, and with no prospect of the "time of alleviation" or that of conditional release. She was quite indomitable, and looked upon all prison officials as her natural enemies to whom she would make no compromise and yield no obedience. Nothing deterred her, no fear of punishment, threats, or infliction of the most irksome conditions, and the whole staff trembled before her.

Elena Rossikova had been sentenced to a life term for a daring robbery from the finance department at Kherson. She was the wife of a country gentleman who had been a school-teacher at Elizabetgrad, and with a confederate she had succeeded in seizing a large sum of public money, meaning to devote it to revolutionary purposes. Her accomplice was Anna Alexieova, afterward Madame Dubrova, a convict and a professional burglar who had escaped from Siberia. They had entered the government treasury through a tunnel driven under the stone floor in the vault of a house adjoining, a wild and desperate scheme for two young and inexperienced girls. That they planned and dared effect it bears witness to the determined character of the Russian women revolutionists. Kennan says the thieves were caught before they could remove all the stolen money, but, according to Leo Deutsch, they succeeded in their attempt. The next day, however, a woman was intercepted as she drove a cart laden with sacks through the town, and the sacks were found to be stuffed full of ruble notes, to the number of a million. Arrest followed, including that of the convict, who at once confessed her share in the transaction and gave such information as led to the recovery of the greater part of the stolen money.

Madame Rossikova, as the elder woman and originator of the plan, was condemned by court-martial, before which she was arraigned, to hard labour for a long term at the mines; Anna Alexieova was sentenced merely to exile as a forced colonist and she married Dubrova, a missionary at Krasnoyarsk. The two girls began as philanthropists, eager to benefit and improve the peasant class, but developed under the persecution of the authorities and their unjust, overbearing treatment into pronounced revolutionists. Both were large-minded women, capable of the greatest self-sacrifice and acting in accordance with a high moral standard. Madame Rossikova had given proof of her sincerity by accepting the ordeal known as "going to the people"; in other words, she lived for seven or eight months like a common peasant woman, in a peasant village, that she might see how best to reach and help the people. She had long disapproved of terrorism, but became a pronounced terrorist herself, moved to the fiercest indignation by the reports that reached her of the sufferings of her exiled friends.

Perhaps one of the most celebrated of the female revolutionists was Madame Vera Phillipova, born Figner, who never found her way to the mines of Kara, where she would undoubtedly have become prominent among the most active champions of her party. She was long the most popular personage in the revolutionary movement; her name was in everybody's mouth, her fine traits, her unfailing and unlimited constancy, her undefeated, self-sacrificing devotion to the cause, her talents for organisation, her boundless inventive powers, her tireless energy,—all won for her profound respect from her comrades; and even her enemies, the members of the court-martial which condemned her, were forced to admire her dignified demeanour when arraigned and tried for her life. A mere girl, of striking beauty, and possessing extraordinary personal influence, she freely spent herself in the service of her fellows. Like many other well-born girls, her chief aim was to help the peasants, and she devoted herself to the rough life in small villages on the Volga, enduring all the hardships and privations of the labouring classes, and her self sacrifice was greatly stimulated by what she saw of misery, poverty and hopeless ignorance.

It was borne in on her that reform could only be effected by the most reckless measures, and she became a terrorist heart and soul, vowed to violence, and prepared to go to any extreme. In this temper, she readily joined in the plot for the assassination of the Czar, Alexander II, on his return from Livadia to St. Petersburg, and the dynamite for use in the bombs was stored in her house. This did not absorb all her energies, and she was still active in the organisation of secret societies and in preaching revolutionary principles among people of good society, to which she belonged by birth and education; for she was the daughter of a distinguished general and was well received by the best people.

At Odessa she mixed much with the military set and thus became identified with the conspiracy of "the Fourteen." Nearly all of those concerned were military or naval officers, five of whom, with Vera Figner and Ludmilla Volkenstein, were condemned to death. She knew that she and her companions had been betrayed, and she might have escaped by timely flight into another country, but she scorned to yield, although arrest was certain, and she held her ground, only to be convicted and thrown into the Schlüsselburg, condemned to imprisonment for the term of her natural life.

Russian Prisoners
After the painting by Marckl

The Fortress of Schlüsselburg is situated on an island in Lake Ladoga, about forty miles from St. Petersburg. The worst of all fates meted out to political prisoners in Russia is imprisonment in the subterranean dungeons of this fortress. No news penetrates the walls of the isolated prison and no information from within leaks out. Few ever leave the prison alive except to be transferred to an insane asylum.

While in the Schlüsselburg, Vera Figner studied Italian and English, and translated many of Kipling's works into Russian. After she had spent altogether twenty years in prison, she committed the offence of striking an officer. Her mother, who had promised not to intercede for her, could no longer keep silent; and appealed to the Czar, with the result that the life sentence passed upon the famous revolutionist was reduced to one of twenty years. Instead of releasing her immediately, however, Plehve kept her two more years in the Schlüsselburg, saying, "There is still too much life left in her." To her unspeakable grief, her mother died a few weeks before she was released in 1904.

She was exiled to a tiny village close to the arctic regions, and a year and a half afterward she was allowed to return to her estate in the Kazan province. She has since made a trip to Italy for her health, and although her nervous system received such a shock that she has never fully recovered, she has renewed activity for the cause to which she has devoted her life by lecturing in foreign cities.

Another woman revolutionist who afterward suffered greatly at Kara was Madame Anna Pavlovna Korba, the daughter of a German nobleman naturalised in Russia, named Meinhardt. She had married a Swiss gentleman living in Russia. She was the friend of Madame Löschern von Herzfeld, who had been one of those banished, but afterward pardoned, in "the case of the 193." She was again arrested at Kiev with arms in her hand, and suffered a second exile with a long imprisonment at Kara. On her return from the campaign of 1878–9 in Turkey, where she had worked as a nurse, she adopted the revolutionary programme. The "white terror" was at its height; the government was active in pursuing the politicals who were pledged to destroy the Czar; and in 1882, Soudyehkin, the chief of the secret police, laid a heavy hand on them, arresting them in batches, executing many and burying the rest alive in St. Petersburg dungeons. Anna Korba, undaunted, threw herself into the fight, and strove earnestly to replace those who had fallen in the ranks. She was arrested for being concerned in the manufacture of dynamite bombs at a secret laboratory, and her trial ended in exile at Kara with twenty years at hard labour, which nearly killed her.

Madame Elizabeth Kovalskaya, whose fruitless effort to escape from Irkutsk has been described, deliberately planned to offend a great official in order to secure her removal. One day, when Baron Korv, the governor-general, visited the prison, she failed purposely to rise from her seat in his presence. Baron Korv objected harshly to this mark of disrespect to a man in his position, and Madame Kovalskaya quietly replied that she had not elected him to it. The enraged official left the prison saying he would send instructions how to deal with this refractory female, and shortly afterward an order came to remove her to the central prison at Verkhni Udinsk, as her unruly behaviour had a demoralising effect at Kara.

The new removal would have been in accordance with Madame Kovalskaya's wishes, but it was most savagely carried out. The blame lay with the commandant of the Kara political prison. Colonel Masyukov, an officer of the gendarmerie, had held this post for about ten years. He was a man of weak character, of low mental calibre, without judgment and quite unfitted for the functions he discharged. Once an officer of the guards, he had wasted his substance in riotous living and had accepted this well paid post to discharge his liabilities and his gambling debts.

Colonel Masyukov stupidly supposed that the female prisoners stirred up by Madame Kovalskaya would have risen to resist her transfer. He resolved, therefore, that she should be conveyed away secretly without a word of notice. A subordinate officer, named Bobrovski, accompanied by a party of gensdarmes and ordinary convicts, burst into her cell at four o'clock in the morning and dragged her out of bed, half naked, with no more covering than her nightdress. She was hurried to the office and here ordered to put on the coarse garments of a common criminal. After this she fainted, and, wrapped up unconscious in a blanket, was carried out to the bank of the river Shilka, where an open boat was in readiness to carry her to Stretensk, the steamboat navigation not being yet practicable. In this small boat she travelled seventy miles for three days and nights with the soldiers of her escort who had already treated her with shameful indignity.

This forcible seizure had aroused the whole prison, and the other women, maddened by the victim's shrieks and believing that her honour was being outraged, became perfectly infuriated. They declared a hunger strike forthwith and refused food unless Masyukov was dismissed from his post. The commandant now deeply regretted his foolish action, and took counsel a little too late from his more sensible subordinates, especially one wise old sergeant, Golubtsov, a tactful man of long experience and much common sense. On his advice the male prisoners were called in to pacify their incensed women comrades and persuade them to abandon their strike. They suggested that the commandant should be requested to apologise to his offended charges, a satisfaction altogether scouted as insufficient by the strikers. The famishing women still insisted upon the withdrawal of Masyukov. The condition seemed impossible of concession by the authorities, but it was hoped that the commandant might himself solve the difficulty by applying for a transfer elsewhere. This settled the question for the moment, and the women consented to take food on the clear understanding that if Masyukov had not disappeared within a certain period, the hunger strike would be recommenced.

This in effect came to pass. The commandant held his ground. The malcontents again refused food, and now the men, although they thought the suggested apology would have been sufficient atonement by Masyukov, joined in the protest and also went out "on strike." The commandant thereupon came to terms; he produced a telegram accepting his resignation; and once more food was eaten, after a week's starvation. But the women would not forgive Masyukov and declined to hold any communication with him. He was "boycotted" completely to the extent even of a refusal on their part to receive their letters from home after passing through his hands. This high spirited resolve reacted very painfully upon themselves. Mental torture worse than the physical was superadded to their sufferings, and they were all but driven to despair. No letters were sent and all which were received were returned unopened through the post to their senders.

This absolute severance of home ties bore especially hard upon one of the latest arrivals in the prison,—Madame Hope Sigida, "a sensitive young creature, gentle, affectionate and attracted by all that was good and beautiful. She was deeply attached to her family, who lived in Taganrock, a small town in South Russia." She had been a school teacher, and was condemned to eight years' hard labour because a printing press and some bombs had been discovered in the house where she resided with her husband who was an officer in Taganrock circuit court. The latter was condemned to death, but the sentence was commuted to deportation to Saghalien, and he died on his way to that island. Madame Sigida, in her bereavement, felt acutely the cessation of all relations with her distant home, and when her comrades, goaded to desperation, were upon the point of resuming the hunger strike, she determined to sacrifice herself for the common good. Hoping that relief might in that way come to the rest, she planned to attack Masyukov alone. She sought an interview with the commandant, and it was granted in due course. A most dramatic incident followed, as told by eye-witnesses. She was driven to the office in a carriage under escort, and was taken in to speak to Colonel Masyukov, who the next moment was seen to jump out of the window, evidently much excited and terrified, and take to his heels. Then Madame Sigida came to the door, and after caressing some warder's children who stood there, in a quiet, unperturbed voice begged that a telegraphic message might be despatched to the proper authorities informing them that she had assaulted the commandant by striking him in the face. She justified her violence as the only means of shaming him into taking his departure. At least she succeeded in forcing him to show himself in his character of a mean, despicable coward.

Madame Sigida was forthwith cast into a secret cell and subjected to "dungeon conditions," while awaiting trial for her grave breach of discipline. Her self-sacrifice had not availed to avert the hunger strike. It began immediately afterward by all the women prisoners, and was persisted in for sixteen days with the same argument, that Colonel Masyukov, now ridiculed and disgraced, must go.

Madame Sigida, still waiting judgment, refused food and remained fasting for twenty-two days, until medical intervention was decreed. Madame Kovalskaya struck the doctor in the face when she thought he was about to forcibly administer nourishment. But he was a humane man and disclaimed all such intention, and she begged his pardon.

For some time no formal inquiry into Madame Sigida's assault was made, and no steps were taken to deal with her case. But after the lapse of a month or more, when the matter had been reported to St. Petersburg, a reply came directed against the whole body of the politicals. Colonel Masyukov, still holding his ground, assembled them and, escorted by soldiers, behind whom he sought protection, read aloud a letter from the governor-general in which he warned the politicals that they were in future amenable to corporal punishment. The penalty was deemed necessary by the authorities for the maintenance of discipline in the disturbed state of the prison.

Consternation fell upon these long suffering victims of a despotic government, who although defenders of their undoubted rights, as admitted in all civilised countries, had never rendered themselves liable to such reprisals. The penalty was, moreover, illegal in their case, and the threat to flog was considered an undeserved and outrageous insult. The desire to raise indignant protest possessed all, and many would have gone so far as to counsel a general suicide. The leader of this extreme view was Sergius Bobohov, a man of the loftiest sentiments, who had adopted revolutionary principles from a strict sense of their justice and necessity. Deutsch's estimate of his character is worth quoting at length. "Genuine sincerity, seriousness of purpose, and boundless devotion to his ideal were his leading traits. He was the most modest of men, but when the honour of a revolutionist was at stake, or if it were a question of duty, he would undergo a transformation and become a fiery and inspired prophet." Bobohov took the threat of flogging very much to heart, and passionately urged that an answering threat of suicide should be addressed to the minister of the interior. "I cling to life as much as any man," he said, "but I am ready to face death as a means of protest." His arguments had weight with his comrades, but might not have prevailed except for the disastrous course of events.

At this moment a catastrophe was precipitated by the almost incredible news that Madame Sigida, the assailant of Colonel Masyukov, was to be flogged by order of Baron Korv, the governor-general and persecutor of Madame Kovalskaya. The punishment was to be inflicted with rods in the presence of the prison doctor, but without previous medical certificate. The surgeon of the Kara penal settlement had given it as his opinion that the poor creature was unfit to receive even a single blow, and declined to be present, as the infliction was by administrative order and without a sentence of court. The governor hesitated to inflict the punishment, but Baron Korv persisted in the flogging, surgeon or no surgeon. The executioner was the same subordinate official, Bobrovski, who had distinguished himself in the misusage of Madame Kovalskaya. He had received promotion for his brutal conduct on that occasion, and was willing to curry favour further with his merciless superiors.

Details of this horrible tragedy are wanting as the lips of those who assisted are sealed. The authorities have, indeed, dared to deny the facts through their mouthpieces in the press, but they were well known throughout Siberia and their truth has been acknowledged by high officials who strove to justify the infliction. Ill-considered attempts have been made by at least imperfectly informed champions to discredit the whole story, which stands nevertheless as an indelible disgrace to Russian penal administrators, whose only excuse was that the nihilist women "had brought troubles upon themselves by being excitable and intractable, and an example was necessary."

So the example was made. Madame Sigida was stripped and beaten with rods, when in a state of unconsciousness, for she soon fainted under the infliction, and was carried back senseless from the place of punishment to her cell. Two days later she died, but whether from the effects of the flogging or from deliberate poisoning is not positively known. Three of her female companions undoubtedly committed suicide, and on the men's side seventeen out of thirty-nine resolved to put an end to their own lives. The result was not altogether successful. The drug, opium, was either old or adulterated, and many who lay down to die only woke to excruciating agony and were saved in spite of themselves. A few of them, Bobohov among the number, tried again, choosing morphia as the means of self-destruction, but once more the drug was ineffective and only two actually died.

The fate of those in durance is largely dependent upon the character and quality of those who have them in charge. Nowhere does this fact stand out more prominently than in Russian prisons. The governor, director or commandant is a petty despot; within his own narrow limits he is almost irresponsible, though subject, of course, to the control of superiors, but this has never been very closely exercised. Inspections are for the most part perfunctory, and abuses, especially that of power, may flourish freely without detection or interference. This ramifies through all the grades, and the prisoner, of whatever class, is very much at the mercy of the subordinate officials with whom he is brought into daily personal contact. The ordinary warder is very much the same everywhere: a man placed in authority over others often superior to himself in antecedents, birth, education and experience of life. He is apt to become arbitrary, tyrannical and self-sufficient from the authority he wields, whether delegated or usurped. After all he is only an agent, a deputy and go-between, carrying out the orders of his masters, whose moods he reflects, whose attitude he imitates, and whose temper animates him, inspiring him to harass and oppress or, more rarely, to be merciful and forbearing. Warders almost invariably take their tone from their supreme chief; hence the deep importance that attaches to the governor in prison life.

There were good and bad rulers in Russian prisons, the latter perhaps predominating, although occasionally a humane, well-intentioned and considerate man was to be met with, such as Kanonovich, who for a time governed the Kara political prison kindly and leniently, as has already been described. After him came a succession of gendarmerie officers from Irkutsk whose characters are summed up by Kennan as follows:—"Khalturin was brutally cruel, Shubin was a man of little character, and Manaiev was not only a drunkard, but a thief who destroyed hundreds of the prisoners' letters and embezzled 1,900 rubles of money sent to them by their relatives and friends in European Russia." Then came Captain Nikolin, of whom more directly. All these were men of much the same stamp as the "Major" of the Omsk *ostrog* described by Dostoyevski. He was, he says, "a fatal being for prisoners, whom he had brought to such a state that they trembled before him. Severe to the point of insanity, 'he threw himself upon them,' to use their expression. But it was above all that look, as penetrating as that of a lynx, that was feared. It was impossible to conceal anything from him. He saw, so to say, without looking. On entering the prison, he knew at once what was being done. Accordingly the convicts, one and all, called him the man with the eight eyes. His system was bad, for it had the effect of irritating men who were already irascible." Fortunately for the prisoners, he was under a superior, for, as the writer tells us, "the commandant was a well-bred, reasonable man who moderated the savage onslaughts of the major, or the latter would have caused sad misfortune by his bad administration."

This major was universally loathed by the prisoners, and more than once was on the verge of murderous attack. There were times when the convicts at Omsk were goaded to desperation by his brutality. One day a dozen men from Little Russia swore to take his life, and their leader had borrowed the kitchen knife and secreted it about his person. The grievance for the moment was the badness of the food, and when the major came in to expostulate, the assailant rushed at him, but found that his victim was drunk, or, according to prison superstition, "under special protection." It was more than he deserved, for he was a blasphemous and overbearing wretch. After having carried the knapsack for many long years, promotion to the grade of officer had turned his head.

Captain Nikolin was an officer of gensdarmes who had been specially selected at St. Petersburg and sent out to govern the state prisons at Kara. Kennan speaks of him as "an old and experienced gendarme officer of the most subtle and unscrupulous type, who had received his training under General Muraviov, 'the hangman, in Poland,' and had been about thirty years in the service.... He had the suavity and courteous manners of the accomplished gendarme officer, ... and he greeted me with what he intended for frank, open cordiality, softening, so far as possible, all the hard lines of his face; but he could not bring a spark of good fellowship into his cold, watchful gray eyes, and I felt conscious that all his real mental processes were carefully masked." He was very proud of his position: that he, a simple captain of gensdarmes, had been sent to this important command, where he was independent of local control and entitled to correspond direct with the minister of the interior. His whole object was to hoodwink Kennan, whom he assured blandly and mendaciously that the prisoners led a life of ease, even of luxury, sitting in a *kamera* like a club smoking room, reading and writing and pleasantly conversing. He further asserted that the "politicals" received considerable sums from their friends in Russia; that they bought what books they pleased, had newspapers, including the London *Punch* and other illustrated papers, and in a word, were "treated with gracious clemency by an enlightened and paternal government." Nikolin showed the cloven foot later when he urged his colleague to seize Mr. Kennan's baggage and search it, by which high-handed proceeding, happily avoided, much of the incriminating material so daringly secured by the fearless American, would have been lost to the indignant readers of the civilised world.

We have another portrait of Captain Nikolin from one who knew him but too well. Leo Deutsch suffered for some years under his régime and describes him "as a malicious, ill-natured man, continually devising petty humiliations for the prisoners." In person he was a short, heavily built man, some fifty years of age, "with a bald head, a full gray beard, thin, tightly closed, rather cruel lips, an impenetrable face and cold gray eyes. His broad round face, cunning little eyes, and bristling moustache, gave him the look of a fat, spiteful old tom-cat, and he was always designated by that nickname. The expression of his eyes was particularly catlike; he looked as if just ready to pounce on a victim and stick his claws into it. He always spoke in a low voice, this 'tom-cat;' but he chattered unceasingly, and kept smacking his lips all the time, his expression being always peevish and discontented.... We petitioned our 'tom-cat' for leave to plant a garden in the yard; there was space enough, the work would have been beneficial, and then we might have had vegetables for our table, the deficiency in which particular had been so detrimental to our health. The 'tom-cat' roundly refused. 'We should need spades,' he said, 'and they might be used to dig a hole whereby to get away.' So, again, when one of us was sent some flower-seeds and sowed them in a wooden box, the box was taken away by Nikolin's orders; the earth in it might have served to conceal some contraband article. Such needless tyrannies embittered us still more against the detested commandant. However peaceably we might otherwise have been inclined, our hatred of this man might well have blazed out at any opportunity; he himself probably guessed as much, for he became more and more mistrustful, at last never entering our prison. He felt that he had made enemies all round him, and sat lonely in his own house, or squabbled with his cook, afraid to show himself outside. It may be a matter of surprise that one of his many enemies did not find a way to put an end to him, that being a not unusual course of events in Kara; but finally he could endure such a life no longer, and applied to be transferred elsewhere. In the spring of 1887 his application was granted, and he departed, accompanied by the anathemas of the entire population of Kara." Captain Nikolin was in due course succeeded by the Colonel Masyukov of whom we have heard so much in his conflict with the politicals of the state prison at Kara.

Captain Nikolin's colleague at Kara, coequal in authority, but with independent functions, was Major Potulov, who governed the ordinary criminal prison at Kara. He was a man of a pleasanter type, who was both civil and hospitable to George Kennan, possibly to keep an eye upon his motions and, perhaps, take the sting out of the condemnation his command so richly deserved. He is described as a tall, fine looking, soldierly man about fifty years of age, affable in manner and disposed to act fairly by his charges, so far as it lay within his power. Where he failed was in loyalty to his superiors, and he was gifted with rare talents for fraud and embezzlement. He stole unblushingly, and enriched himself largely at the expense of the state. His chief device was to keep hundreds of prisoners on the rolls who were mere "ghosts;" men who had disappeared by flight or death, but for whom rations were still drawn and the value thereof shared between him and the purveyor. He was presently detected and dismissed, but escaped justice through his influential friends.

Patrin of Saghalien came to the front at a later date, when deportation to the island colony was in full swing, and his evil reputation became widespread as the most brutal and rapacious official in Russian penal annals. His character was so well known far and wide that he figured as the prison demon on the San Francisco stage. His was a reign of terror in the Alexandrovsk prison, and he drove through the town armed with revolver and Winchester rifle, committing acts of atrocious criminal violence in the open streets. Horrible stories were current of his misusage of his charges, of constant punishments in the dark cells or with the plet till death was the result. He was equally harsh with his officers. One of them, who had gone to complain of the insulting and outrageous conduct of a comrade toward his (the complainant's) wife, was struck on the mouth by Patrin and felled to the ground. He had an abrupt way of dealing with recalcitrant prisoners. One day there came before him a young convict of an irascible temper, who had obstinately refused to work. Patrin forthwith fell upon him, striking him on the jaw. The prisoner, although of slight build, closed with the governor and, showing superhuman strength, dragged him to the top of the staircase. Now the warders who had been hanging about hurried to their chief's assistance, and the fight became a perfect mêlée in one confused struggling group, all gravitating toward the edge of the stairs, down which they suddenly fell headlong. Patrin came out on top, with the prisoner underneath. But the latter had seized a revolver from one of the guards, and when he was raised to his feet pointed the weapon to his own forehead and shot himself, saying, "It was Patrin I wanted to kill."

The political prisoners at Saghalien were subjected to the tender mercies of Patrin, and he also had charge of the women's prison, but his infamous behaviour toward the women was too abominable to be told.

CHAPTER IX
CHANGES IN SYSTEM

The Kara settlements—Descriptions of the prisons by Kennan—Filthy state of the prison buildings at Ust Kara—Gold mining—Illicit trade in "stolen gold"—Improvements in the prison system—The new prison of Alexandrovsk—Mr. Foster Fraser's account of the excellent state of the prison in 1901—The prison at Verkhni Udinsk—The island of Saghalien used as a penal colony—Disadvantages of the place—Coal mining chief industry—Climate uncongenial—Exiles sent by sea from Odessa—Terrible sufferings on the voyage—Convict marriages—Deplorable conditions on the island—Prison discipline in force at Alexandrovsk—Punishments inflicted—The plet.

Of the partial attempts made by Russia to reform the methods of inflicting penal servitude on wrong-doers, I shall speak more at large. A detailed account must be given of the new prisons erected more in conformity with modern ideas; and the persistent pursuit of that will-o'-the-wisp, penal colonisation by deportation to the desert island of Saghalien, with its futile processes and disappointing results, claims attention. Before leaving the older methods of enforcing hard labour, it will be well to describe its last stronghold and the system obtaining there until quite a recent date. "Kara the Black," so called from a Tartar word, aptly describes the series of prisons and convict settlements established in the valley of the Kara River to work the mines, chiefly gold mines, the private property of the Czar. There are other mines of salt and silver, the latter chiefly at Nertchinsk, supposed to have been worked out, and now leased to private hands with profitable return, in spite of their deadly unhealthiness from the quicksilver emanations that poisoned them. The annals of Nertchinsk are as horrible as any in Siberian prison history, and the ancient prison of Akatui in the district still stands to bear witness to the cruelties and tragedies practised upon the unhappy politicals who inhabited it. The silver mines were reopened at Algachi in the neighbourhood, where there was a prison which Kennan saw and unhesitatingly condemned. "As a place of confinement," he writes, "even for the worst class of offenders, it was a disgrace to a civilised state, and the negligence, indifference and incompetence shown by the government in dealing with its admitted evils were absolutely inexcusable." Speaking further of the Nertchinsk district and of the mines at Algachi and Pokrovski and others, Mr. Kennan was of opinion that the prisoners permitted to work in them suffered less than those, the larger proportion, who were doomed to unbroken idleness in the overcrowded, foul-smelling prisons. It was irksome enough to work eight or ten hours daily in an icy gallery, three hundred feet below ground; the mines were badly ventilated, and the gases liberated by the explosives used may be injurious; but there are no deadly exhalations from poisonous ores to affect the health, and no doubt the worst feature of penal servitude in Siberia was not the hard labour in the mines but the almost inconceivably foul condition and enforced idleness of the prisons.

Returning now to the Kara prisons, seven in number, two of them were allotted to politicals, one for each sex, and of the remaining five the total population was approximately eighteen hundred convicts. Half of them were detained as prisoners; the other half were permitted generally to join the "free command." The latter were still convicts, receiving rations and restricted to the settlement, but residing in barracks or in their own houses. The prison building of Ust Kara, at the Lower Diggings, is compared by Kennan to "a long, low, horse-car stable made of squared but unpainted logs, which are now black, weather-beaten, and decaying from age." It was in the form of a square surrounded by logs twenty-five feet high, closely set together, and sharpened at the top like enormous lead pencils. Entrance was gained after ascending a few steps through a heavy wooden door opening upon a long, low and very dark corridor with a wet, slippery floor, much broken and damaged. The first sensation was that of damp air laden with the fetid odours that constantly vitiate all Siberian prisons. Kennan was unable to compare it to any known bad smell. He says, "I can ask you to imagine cellar air, every atom of which has been half a dozen times through human lungs and is heavy with carbonic acid; to imagine that air still further vitiated by foul, pungent, slightly ammoniacal exhalations from long unwashed human bodies.... To unaccustomed senses, it seems so saturated with foulness and disease as to be almost insupportable. As we entered the corridor, slipped upon the wet, filthy floor, and caught the first breath of this air, Major Potulov (the commandant) turned to me with a scowl of disgust, and exclaimed, 'It is a repulsive prison.'" In the cells there was absolutely no ventilation whatever. Even the brick oven drew its air from the corridor. The walls of squared logs had once been whitewashed, but had become dark and grimy, and were blotched in many places with extensive bloodstains, the life blood of countless insatiable enemies, bed-bugs, crushed to death in unceasing warfare. The floor was deeply encrusted with dry, hard-trodden filth. The sloping wooden platforms on which the convicts slept side by side, closely packed, without bedding or covering, were inconceivably dirty. All the cells were the same except that in one a shoemaker's bench diffused the quite pleasing odour of fresh leather.

Small wonder that contagious diseases were rife in such an atmosphere; scurvy, typhus and typhoid constantly prevailed and the prison surgeon admitted that the first was endemic, saying, "We have more or less scurvy here all the year round." The infected were not at once removed to hospital, but lay there to pollute and poison the air breathed by their comparatively healthy comrades. All the conditions of this were so manifestly odious that the commandant did not attempt to explain, defend or excuse them, but, as Kennan tells us, "he grew more and more silent, moody and morose as we went through the *kameras*." He knew too well that it was beyond his power to remedy the abounding evil; he might listen to grievances, hear petitions and complaints, but was powerless to relieve them.

The middle Kara prison was on precisely similar lines, but the air was fresher during the day time, when the bulk of the inmates were absent at the mines, to which the hard-labour prisoners proceeded in the early morning and where they spent the day. Their midday meal was taken with them, to be eaten beside the camp fire in any weather, even the fiercest winter storms. They returned to the prison late in the afternoon, and dined on a fairly good meal of hot soup, bread and meat and a cup of brick tea. This they ate on their sleeping platforms, and passed the night without removing their clothing.

The gold "placers" at Kara were generally in deep gravel pits, and the auriferous sand was located beneath a stratum of clay, gravel or stones, in what had once been the bed of the stream. The work consisted in breaking up and removing this overlying stratum, extracting the gold bearing sand and carrying it to the machine, where it was washed in several waters which in flowing away left deposits of black sand and gold particles. Pick and crowbar were in constant use by the convict labourers, working in their leg irons silently and listlessly under the close surveillance of a cordon of Cossack sentries. The average daily task was of ten hours, but much time was lost in going to and fro, and the annual amount washed was some four hundred pounds. A large quantity of gold was stolen by the surreptitious washing of convicts of the free command. They disposed of it to "receivers," who ran great risks but generally managed to smuggle it across the frontier. This illicit trade flourishes in spite of the fact that it is a penal offence to be in possession of the precious metal or "golden wheat," as it is technically called. But the great profits accruing outbalance the risks, and small speculators are always to be found who will secretly buy the stolen treasure secured by the convicts at large.

One notorious criminal at Kara living in the free command acquired considerable wealth by illicit trade in "stolen gold." His name was Lissenko, and his crimes had been many and heinous. In one of his robberies he murdered a whole family, men, women and children. Leo Deutsch came across him and describes him as a man of about sixty years who had still the strength of a giant. He says: "He struck me as being crafty, cunning and reckless, but not a malicious kind of fellow, and he was extremely pious withal. No one who knew him personally could easily believe him to have murdered innocent children." Deutsch asked him how he could have the heart to kill a child. "Oh, I cried all the time I was doing it," he replied, "but still I killed them. It was just God's will." His questioner then asked, "Well, and would you murder me if you met me in a safe place?" "If I knew you had a lot of money about you I should certainly wring your neck," said the man, with cheerful frankness. "But there! one doesn't kill without some good reason."

The search for gold, belonging really to the government, or more exactly to the Czar, was almost openly practised at Kara. Whole families, both men and women, engaged in it, taking out with them a shovel and wooden vessel to the banks of the neighbouring streams, and often obtaining gold dust to the value of a couple of rubles a day. No one protested, and the authorities hardly interfered, for the officials themselves did not scruple to profit by the illegal trade. Far more gold was obtained by unlawful than lawful means. The middlemen got a good price from the Chinese traders, who could always find a way to pass the gold into China, where it would fetch a higher price than that paid by the imperial exchequer. It is contended that these illicit gold finders have greatly benefited Siberia. Their restless energy in prospecting has led to the discovery of numberless gold mines, which are now being very profitably worked, seldom to the enrichment of the finders, but to that of the middlemen and through them to that of the country.

The glaring shortcomings of Eastern Siberian prisons were gradually recognised by the government, and a commendable, if not extensive, attempt has been made to provide new and improved buildings, both to serve as forwarding prisons, and for the confinement of penal-servitude convicts. A larger scheme was introduced for the penal colonisation of the island of Saghalien by the deportation of exiles thither by sea, of which I shall have much more to say. The best of the new prisons on the mainland are those of Alexandrovsk, forty miles above Irkutsk on the Amgara River, of Gorni Zerentui at the Nertchinsk mines, and of Verkhni Udinsk, fifty miles east of Lake Baikal and six hundred miles from Kara.

The prison of Alexandrovsk, which was visited by the untiring investigator, Kennan, had been originally built to serve as a distillery, but was reconstructed and turned into a great central prison in 1874. When Kennan was there, it held about a thousand prisoners and was deemed to be almost a model prison. It is a large two-storied brick building with a tin roof, standing in a spacious enclosure surrounded by a high, buttressed brick wall. It contains fifty-seven general cells, in each of which from five to seventy-five occupants are locked up; ten cells for separate confinement, and five secret cells for the isolation of the most dangerous and refractory prisoners. The cells, as Kennan found, were large and lofty; the ventilation was good and the air pure; floors and sleeping rooms were kept scrupulously clean, the only fault in the latter being the absence of bedding. The corridors outside the cells were spacious, well lighted, and the air was wholesome. Neatness, cleanliness and good order prevailed in the great kitchen; the food prepared was palatable and good. The daily rations per week consisted of three pounds of rye bread, seven ounces of meat, three ounces of barley, with potatoes and other vegetables occasionally. The prisoners were permitted to purchase tea and sugar out of their own earnings and private funds. A schoolroom, well furnished and supplied, existed in the prison, and there were many citizens' shops,—carpenters, shoemakers, and tailors,—and two-thirds of the money earned was at the disposal of the handicraftsmen. Other labour intended to be "hard" was enforced at the mills, where rye seed was ground into meal and where the prisoners worked for three or four hours daily. At night the *kamera* was crowded and dimly lighted; and when visited, was not quite so sweet and odourless as during the daytime, but, on the whole, the prison was infinitely superior to the foul dens already described.

Mr. Foster Fraser, the English traveller, who saw the Alexandrovsk central prison in 1901–2, gives a no less favourable report. He describes it as a great square building, with lofty corridors, colour washed, and with sanded floors, the *kameras* containing on an average fifty men each. The prisoners, who hailed from all parts of the polyglot and scattered Russian Empire, were criminals of the worst stamp, mostly heavy-jowled, sullen, brutish men, but there were some few young and innocent looking lads. In the cells large numbers lounged away the day in complete idleness, but all asked for employment, and were glad to get it by being taken into the various shops. Some were clever and skilful at particular trades, cabinet-making, tailoring, bookbinding, designing patent locks, watch-mending or making musical instruments. The impression conveyed was that of workshops of well contented artisans. Conversation was general and many were smoking cigarettes. Care was taken to classify prisoners by their religions; Mahometans, Tartars and Caucasians were kept together in one hall; Jews were in another with their synagogue hard by. The desire to brighten the gloomy surroundings was to be seen in the existence of a theatre with stage and scenery, where excellent amateur performances were given, and also musical entertainments, for singing was much cultivated and there was no lack of good voices among the convicts. A large library was kept up, to which free access was permitted for several hours daily to those who could read, by no means a large proportion.

There is a second Alexandrovsk prison, one of the *étapes*, or forwarding prisons, newly built in 1886–8, and on good lines, but much handicapped by the common blot on all such places, overcrowding. Great numbers, far in excess of available accommodation, were collected here, awaiting distribution to various points. Mr. Fraser's verdict on this *étape* prison is unfavourable.

"The rooms were overcrowded and the stench almost choked me. The men looked dirty and uncared for. They had no work; they were just huddled together, waiting often six or eight months before they were sent off. Among them were half a dozen young fellows in ordinary clothes, with nothing of the criminal about them, the youngest seventeen, the eldest twenty-one. They were political exiles banished by 'administrative process' for rashly joining in some socialistic demonstration, and were on their way to Yakutsk into the frozen depths of the sub-Arctic Circle."

Verkhni Udinsk is the first halting place after leaving Lake Baikal on the road to Kara, and all exiles to Eastern Siberia passed through it, including the political prisoners. For many years the *étape* prison there was one of the foulest on the whole route. It is to the credit of the Russian government that this abominable prison has been abolished and replaced (in 1886) by a new forwarding prison constructed on the most approved lines. It is a large building of four stories, built of brick, with a stucco front painted white, and having two spacious wings, a large inner courtyard and separate buildings for political prisoners and military guard. The *kameras* are even better than those at Alexandrovsk, large, lofty, well ventilated, and each above the basement floor has an extensive view across the surrounding country through at least three large windows. The corridors and imposing staircases, and even the solitary confinement cells, are of large size. It was built to lodge 440, but of course was constantly occupied by a much larger number. When Mr. Kennan expressed his unbounded approval of the very best prison he had seen in Russia, or indeed in any country, his conductor assented, "Yes; if they do not overcrowd it, it will be very comfortable. But as the old prison intended for 140 was often filled with as many as seven hundred, we shall probably be expected to find room for three thousand in this." I have come across no later information on this point, and it is to be hoped that the substitution of the sea passage to Saghalien has had a beneficial effect in reducing the numbers passing along the land route, and that the Verkhni Udinsk prison has sufficed to meet the demands on its accommodation.

After very considerable delay, a new prison at Gorni Zerentui, to serve for the Nertchinsk mines, was completed in 1888. The crying need for such a prison was first realised in 1872, and in 1874 a committee was appointed to report and submit plans. Seven years later no more progress had been made than the erection of a few log huts and the repair of some older buildings, on which nearly 40,000 dollars had been expended. Constant changes of plan had tended to vexatious delay. Opinions were divided as to whether brick or logs was the most suitable material, but preference was finally given to the latter, because the prison could not be permanent, as the mines were certain to become worked out. But already brick had been employed and the building was far forward, so it was at length completed, and was occupied at the date given.

The advantages offered by the island of Saghalien as a place for penal settlement were very early impressed upon Russian prison administrators. They were rather sentimental than physical, for the island was perhaps as unsuitable for human habitation as any place on the face of the globe. The climate was uncongenial, and worse even than its latitude indicated. Alexandrovsk, the chief town, is in the same latitude as Brighton in England, and yet its mean annual temperature is just below freezing point. No sea current wafted any warmth northward from Chinese waters. On the contrary, a bitterly cold stream swept its eastern coast, issuing from the ice-bound sea of Okhotsk, and the western shores of this narrow elongated island are, so to speak, under an immense refrigerator, the snowy mountain tracts of Siberia, separated from it by only a narrow and shallow channel. Sparse sunlight pierced through the heavy clouds and fogs that enveloped this inhospitable land. The milder season was too brief to allow of great success in the germination of crops, and the long, low valleys between the mountains were too damp and marshy to favour agriculture. Dense forests clothed a large portion of the island, containing poor trees of inferior, stunted growth, with comparatively valueless wood. A scant population of degenerate tribes eked out a wretched existence as fishermen and seal hunters. Few settlers came to it from China or Japan.

The report of experts definitely decided against Saghalien as an agricultural colony. The soil forbade all hope of raising grain to support those who worked it. Food must be imported to maintain life; cattle breeding might succeed, but with difficulty, and fish must remain the staple diet. One source of natural wealth which might be developed was the coal fields, in which the island was supposed to be rich, but the quality of the coal was inferior to the Australian and very much below that of Newcastle and Cardiff. Mr. Hawes, a later traveller (1903), contests this, however, and describes the coal as a good lignite, superior to the Japanese as a steam coal, and says it commands a higher price. As an article of commerce, it suffers from the difficulties of lading for export. There is not a single harbour on the whole circumference of the island, and approach is often hindered by want of beacons and constantly prevailing fogs.

Coal mining in Saghalien began in 1858, and some 30,000 tons were extracted during the first ten years. The production was very costly; the mines were worked by candle light; the ore was bad and much mixed with stone. The largest deposits are upon the western coast, and it is mined chiefly at Dui and Vladiminsk. Mr. Hawes saw a seam of brown coal exposed on the banks of the river Tim. At Vladiminsk the coal was on the ground, level, and easily reached by tunnelling into the cliff, and when it failed at one spot, another was soon discovered. The coal sells to the merchants at twelve shillings per ton, of which the convicts now employed receive ten per cent.

The adoption of Saghalien as a penal colony commended itself to the authorities for several reasons. In the first place, the conditions of life were more irksome than on the mainland; the work would, it was thought, be much harder; and the place itself was wilder, more savage and solitary,—all of which would combine to increase the severity of the punishment. Moreover, the prospect of remaining forever as a settler upon a remote island, after the term of hard labour was accomplished, would still further act as a deterrent to crime. Accordingly, it was resolved to inflict this harsher penalty upon recidivists and recaptured fugitives, the *brodyagi*, or runaway convicts, of whom so many thousands were always at large and who, when recaptured, as well as all the "Ivan-don't-remembers" who would not tell their names, were sentenced to penal servitude for a fresh term of four years in Saghalien. Again, Saghalien by sea was better than Siberia by *étape* process, with its long painful journey, the sufferings it entailed on the travellers, and the burden of corruption inflicted upon the local population by the way. Last of all, it would tend to free Siberia of the convict element, and assist the colonisation and development of the new territory, with manifest benefit to the convicts on release by the opportunities offered for rehabilitation and betterment of character and position.

These were the views expressed by Governor-General Anuchin in his famous reports to the Czar in 1880. But they had already taken effect, and deportation to Saghalien had begun practically some years previously. The first body of convicts, eight hundred in number, were sent there in 1869, but they went across the whole continent of Asia, having already travelled from Russia, and descending the long length of the Amur River, some two thousand miles, completed a total journey of 4,700 miles before reaching its mouth at Nikolaevsk, where they arrived decimated by disease and all more or less suffering from scurvy. After that, sea transportation was used, the party starting from Odessa and voyaging through the Suez Canal by the Red Sea, Indian and Northern Pacific Oceans, but under very neglected and imperfect conditions, so that those who embarked were subjected to terrible privations and cruelties on this voyage half round the world.

As time passed, and the last century drew to its close, deportation direct to Saghalien steadily increased. Twice a year the steamer *Yaroslav*, one of the Russian volunteer fleet, the appointed convict ship, performed its sad mission and brought out its living freight of eight hundred exiles from Odessa. Besides these, many hundreds regularly arrived from the mainland, who were convicts due to become exiled settlers. The latest law provided that the penal colony should be the receptacle of all males sentenced to more than two years, of all females not over forty years of age, sentenced to the same period, and of any political prisoner at the discretion of the imperial government. Criminals, on arrival, are classified according to their sentences and located in the various gaols in the three administrative districts of Alexandrovsk, Timovsk and Korsakovsk. The largest prison centre is at the first named; the second in importance is at Korsakovsk; and there are two prisons in the Timovsk district, one at Derbensk, the other at Rikovsk.

When Mr. Hawes visited the island in 1902, he found a principal gaol at Alexandrovsk known as the "testing," or probation prison, for the worst criminals, those with a sentence of twelve years and upward, whose fetters are not removed and who are confined in a quarter styled the "chained" prison. There is a second prison known as the "reformatory," for those with lesser sentences, into which convicts from the testing prison, after passing a minimum of four years, may be promoted. These last-named prisoners are permitted to work in gangs beyond the walls, under escort, without very strict discipline, so that many leave their parties to work on their own account in various forms of depredation. The "ticket-of-leave" men, or free commands, were entered on the lists of the reformatory prison and included the vagrants, *brodyagi*, who were deported after recapture on the mainland. Immediate release from jail is the boon conceded to any convict, even the very worst, whose freeborn wife has elected to come out from Russia and join him. He becomes then an exile settler of one of the "peasant" class, so-called, whom it is hoped will assist colonisation. The same boon is conceded to female convicts. "Free" husbands, however, are not often eager to share their lot. According to Mr. Hawes, there were only six of these loyal spouses on the whole island. But the women convicts have the chance of being chosen to join in a convict marriage or temporary coupling of parties, which is not only permitted but strongly encouraged. The consequences of such unions are deplorable. The effect on the woman is most demoralising, and too often the offspring, when children are born, have inherited the criminal taint. The civil contract cannot be entered into without divorce in the case where a husband still exists in Russia, although many widows have simplified the matter by murdering their husbands before leaving home, often, indeed, the cause of their deportation. Figures quoted for one year, 1897, show that there were 2,836 murderers in durance upon the island, and a much larger number if ex-convicts were included, and of this total, 634 were women who had murdered their husbands. Clergymen on Saghalien refused to give a religious sanction to these civil contracts unless there had been a formal dissolution of the Russian marriage. The civil bond sat lightly on both parties; the women in particular elected to go their own way, and if interfered with or if they found their marriage ill-assorted or irksome, they at once transferred themselves to some other master. The results of this outrage upon the most sacred of human institutions must assuredly lead to its abolition; they are identically the same as reported by Mr. George Griffith to be the case in New Caledonia.

He says: "I saw about seventy-six separate and distinct reasons for the abolition of convict marriages at the convict school. On every face and form were stamped the unmistakable brand of criminality, imbecility, moral crookedness and general degeneration."

The testing prison at Alexandrovsk generally held some six hundred inmates, many of them in chains and most of them in idleness; a few, barely ten or twelve per cent., were occasionally sent out to be employed in mining, road-making and log-hauling; and the authorities justified this limitation by the plea that the majority of them were such desperate characters that they could not safely be suffered to go beyond the walls. The unutterable weariness of long-continued, unbroken idleness bore so heavily upon this mass of caged and shackled humanity that desperate and determined attempts at escape were of constant occurrence. So great was their longing to be free that they would willingly risk their lives to breathe the fresh air. The only break in the dull round of prison life was surreptitious gambling. They would sacrifice everything to secure the means of play; they would stake the government clothing issued, and even their rations a month ahead. In the latter case, as an alternative to punishment, the convict put himself in pawn to the authorities. He was lodged in a separate cell and allowed himself to be starved for two days out of every three; the rations saved were accumulated and placed to his credit for the payment of his debt.

The conditions of life at Alexandrovsk not strangely incited the prisoners to turbulence, insubordination and the commission of crime whenever the chance came. When at large, even for a short time after successful escape, they were veritable brigands, robbing and slaughtering; when once more incarcerated, they were intractable and incorrigible, and no punishment could affright or keep them in order.

The older brutal methods survive in Saghalien. Physical tortures are superadded to the infliction of prolonged sentences. As to the latter, many convicts are well advanced in life with unexpired sentences of forty or fifty years. Hawes tells us he found thirteen in this class, and fifty-one others, one of them a woman, with sentences of from thirty to forty years, and 240 with from twenty to thirty years of unexpired sentences. He also found a couple of offenders chained to wheelbarrows, and the number had been much larger not long before.

Employment of corporal punishment has for the most part disappeared in Russian and Siberian prisons; its infliction at Kara on Madame Sigida in 1889, and the universal horror inspired throughout the civilised world by this terrible catastrophe, largely led to its abandonment; but the practice is still in force in Saghalien. Until 1902 females were flogged with the *rozgi*, birch rods dipped in salt. The infliction was within the power of the chief of the prison, and although it might be lightly, was ever arbitrarily imposed. It was not an excessively cruel, but a most brutal and disgraceful punishment. But the plet still flourishes, although the leaded ends are said to have been replaced by knots, and may be a very terrible weapon in the hands of a skilful flagellator. Until recently, it was worthy to replace the murderous knout of ancient times. The patient was very much at the mercy of the executioner, the so-called *palach*, a salaried convict-official, to whom his comrades paid tribute in the Saghalien prison in food and tobacco, to curry favour with him and persuade him to lay the leaded ends of the lash so as to catch the wooden flogging bench rather than their bare backs. The *palach* spared his victim at very considerable risk, and might be flogged for neglect of duty. In one case, an offending executioner, by name Komeleva, was punished and flogged by the hands of his particular enemy. So terrible was the infliction that although it incurred in 1882, a photograph taken of the wounds in 1899, seventeen years afterwards, showed them to be still suppurating. Three strokes of the plet were sufficient to kill, and another story is told of a convict at Saghalien who promised the *palach* a bottle of vodka if he would not hit him with the leaded ends. The victim was a hardened veteran, and when he had received ninety-five strokes, thinking he had escaped, he called out, "It's no matter; you can't hurt me now, you needn't think you'll get your vodka." But he had not reckoned with his man, for after three more strokes he was dead. It was only necessary to draw back the plet as the stroke was spent for the ends to injure the liver and send a clot of blood to the heart.

CHAPTER X
SAGHALIEN

Failure of the scheme to utilise Saghalien as a convict settlement—Testimony of an official on the terrible condition of the exiles—Gambling and drunkenness universal—Prevalence of immorality—The prisons hot beds of vice—No classification of the prisoners—Convicts refuse to settle on the island as colonists at the expiration of their sentence—Account of two assassinations at Alexandrovsk—Description of the cemetery there—Female murderers on the island—Sophie Bluffstein, called the "Golden Hand"—Her adventurous career of crime—Sent to Saghalien as a political prisoner—Carried on criminal operations when released—Recaptured and again confined—Finally released and settled on the island until her death—The merchant of Alexandrovsk and his unfaithful wife—The vagrants in Saghalien—Barratasvili—His capture and death—Horrible story of the fate which befell the convict road-makers—Politicals on Saghalien—Their terrible sufferings.

The day will come when Russia, like the rest of the world, will learn that it cannot finally dispose of its worst elements by shooting them down on some distant dust heap. Siberia will act in its own defence as did Australia, and refuse to be forever the dumping ground for criminals. The prosperous development of that vast and richly endowed territory has been too long delayed and already a change is imminent. Enterprise has been stimulated by the construction of the great Trans-Siberian railway. As Siberia grows in wealth and importance it will surely resent and repudiate the exile system, whether enforced by the improved methods of railway travelling or facilitated by sea communications.

The old idea of removal still obtains, although an effort has been made to avoid the horrors of the prolonged pilgrimage on land, by substituting the long sea voyage from Odessa, through the Suez canal and the southern seas to far Saghalien. Banishment to that convict colony, although half the island has passed to the victorious Japanese, will still survive, despite its manifest failure.

After the experience of a quarter of a century, it may be most unhesitatingly asserted that the net result of the deportation to Saghalien has been most disappointing. Failure has met the Russian government on every side. Transportation has fulfilled none of the aims of penal legislation, has been neither reformatory nor deterrent, but merely painful and punitive without any return in benefit to the colony. The island has made no progress; its scanty natural resources have been little utilised, and no return has been obtained from the cultivation of the indifferent soil. At the best period, barely one-tenth of the convicts qualifying for conditional freedom, and labouring to become proprietors of farms with lands cleared and stocked with cattle, were of any value in carrying on the work; of the remaining nine-tenths, half had no heart in it, and the other half were frankly idlers and vagabonds hanging about the settlements, looking for free rations, and when the issue ceased, ranging the country as masterless men depending on theft and depredation for their bare living.

The social atmosphere was vitiated, and noxious evil elements predominated; general depravity had become almost universal. It was the old story of Australian transportation, and the later experience of New Caledonia. Once more, penal exile stands condemned as a secondary punishment, showing the same absence of any redeeming or compensating features in the improvement of these new lands or the amelioration of the individual. The system must be still more barren of results in the future, now that the southern half of the island—the part most favourable to agriculture—has been surrendered to Japan as part of the last war indemnity. This will seriously diminish the amount of land available for the "exile settlers," as they are called.

The efforts made to colonise have been feeble and fruitless. Convict labourers were set to clear the forests and reclaim waste lands, but in a desultory, half-hearted fashion, without skill or knowledge, and wielding primitive instruments and imperfect tools. Much time was wasted in covering long distances to draw rations, and depending upon the administration for advances to provide seed and stock, both inadequate in quantity and of very inferior quality. As a general rule, the settlers were physically unfit for the work in hand; their health was not robust; they soon aged and broke down under the rough conditions of daily life. All were crushed with indebtedness to the government for advances, and also to private usurers who supplied means for self-indulgence. A fierce passion for gambling consumed them, and drunkenness was universal. Vodka was smuggled in freely from Japan, and numbers of illicit stills manufactured it secretly upon the island. One of the principal officials spoke as follows of the deplorable state of things:—

"Convict life on Saghalien is a frightful nightmare. It is a compound of debauchery, insolence and bravado, mixed with real suffering from hardship and privation, and tainted indelibly with crime and corruption." Children born on or brought to the island are educated in the worst vices, and when still of tender years are already profligate or depraved. Modesty does not exist; young girls of twelve and thirteen are invariably seduced and abandoned to prostitution; men enter into the civil marriage so as to profit by the immorality of their temporary wives; many female convicts are retained in government hands, simply to purvey concubines for the colonial officials. The unsavoury and shameless relations of the sexes are among the principal reasons why colonisation has absolutely failed. There is no virtue among the female residents of Saghalien, whether they are "free" women who have come out voluntarily to join husbands or parents, or those condemned to deportation. The latter are in many respects better placed than the former, for they receive government shelter and allowances in food.

The prisons on the island are hot-beds of vice; all classes of offenders are herded together, with no system of classification but the one based upon the length of sentence. An attempt has been made to separate the uncondemned awaiting trial from the recidivist and hardened offender, but the division is not carried far, and too often the association is indiscriminate, and the wholly bad habitual criminals mix freely with the less hardened wrongdoers, who are rapidly corrupted and debased by their evil surroundings. The worst elements are concentrated in the "testing" prison of Alexandrovsk, including those who have graduated and grown gray in crime on the mainland. Prison discipline is generally slack and ineffective, and from ill-judged economy the staff of warders is too weak for supervision and control. The officers themselves are often of inferior stamp, drunken, untrustworthy, overbearing, given to "trafficking" with the prisoners, accepting bribes for the clandestine introduction of strong drink, or to assist in escapes, quick to oppress and misuse their charges.

Another impediment to colonisation is the noted and invincible dislike to the place constantly present in the minds of the enforced colonists or exiled class at large. No ex-convict would willingly remain on Saghalien. When their terms of detention are ended, all want to turn their backs on the island forever. Nothing would reconcile one to continued residence, not even the acquisition of comparative wealth and the possession of lands and herds, a house to shelter him, and domestic ties. Anyone who can happily scrape together the necessary means hungers to spend it in paying his passage home. He must possess his soul in patience for a long time. Six years must be spent as an exile settler after release from his prison probation; six more as a peasant, and then only permission is granted to cross to the mainland, but never to return to St. Petersburg or Moscow. Now and again a fugitive—and there is a large percentage of escapes as we shall see—may reach home, but he is in constant danger of rearrest. One political prisoner actually succeeded in reaching the capital, but had the bad luck to meet in the streets of St. Petersburg a gendarme officer who knew him. He was recognised and sharply interrogated. "How did you manage to come so far, and what brings you here?" asked the officer. "This brought me," replied the exile, as he promptly drew his revolver and shot his inconvenient questioner down. Arrest followed immediately, and trial, with a fresh sentence of fifteen years. Once more he was sent to Saghalien, where he is still living as an exile settler with small hope of a second enlargement.

There are occasional, but very rare, exceptions among ex-convicts who elect to remain and settle down in the colony. Mr. Hawes tells us of one, a Cossack from the Caucasus, probably an old insurgent, who, with tireless industry, had made himself a home at the village of Uskovo on the upper waters of river Tim, some fifty miles from Alexandrovsk. This man with infinite labour had cleared enough of the primeval forest to sow a respectable crop of corn, some 150 puds or upwards of 5,000 English pounds, which returned him a twelvefold crop. He was a careful farmer, and sowed his seed with judgment, unlike most of the peasants who scattered it at one place insufficiently and at another in excess. Yet good harvests might be secured by steady industry, were the peasants only willing to give agriculture a fair trial. Another similar case was that of a free-command convict, whose wife had followed him out from Europe. He was permitted to live with her outside the prison on condition that he performed his allotted task of hard labour, which was to haul tree trunks into Alexandrovsk to the number of one hundred and twenty. He was energetic and thrifty, and by the aid of a loan from the crown purchased a number of draught ponies to help him in hauling, by which means he contrived to get a certain amount of spare time to work on his own account. He had struck a new idea, inspired by the fact that a steady traffic in oxen and ponies, bound to the town bazaar or market, constantly passed his door. He established a sort of livery stable in a little courtyard adjoining his cottage, where he provided shelter for the cattle and sleeping places for the drovers on beds of hay. He soon did a large business and prospered greatly.

Sometimes there was a sad slip between the cup and the lip. It is on record that an exile settler by unremitting diligence had put by enough to pay for his passage home at the expiration of his term of exile. On his way to Alexandrovsk, he was resting on a bridge when another villager of the free command came and seated himself alongside. Suddenly, as they chatted pleasantly together, the newcomer knocked the other senseless with a heavy blow on the head, and having rifled his body, dropped it into the stream running below. He thus became possessed of his victim's pocket-book containing his money and the certificate of the expiration of his sentence. Fate was adverse, however, and when he proceeded to make use of his ill-gotten gains, the certificate was recognised as the property of the deceased. Arrest and detention were followed by full discovery of the crime and its punishment.

At Saghalien there was no security to life and property in the towns and still less safety in the interior, which was ravaged and harassed by the vagrant convicts, continually moving to and fro. Murder was committed daringly and unblushingly on the smallest temptation, such as the possession of even a small sum of money. When Mr. Hawes was at Alexandrovsk, he met when on his way to church a couple of men just out of hospital who had evidently been drinking. One of them reeled a little in his walk and was manifestly drunk. Within a few hours this luckless creature lay, a corpse, in the market place. He had been murdered by his companion for the six or seven rubles he carried in his pocket. Three days later, a man living near the market place imprudently sat near the lamp at an open window, and was shot through it. Hawes describes the cemetery he visited on a hill to the north of the town; it was filled with wooden crosses, black, brown and green, clustering thickly, and much the same epitaph was inscribed on all, "Here lies —— murdered —— 18—." No mention was made of the assassin; that was quite unnecessary. The victims were buried both singly and in groups of three, four or five. The theatre of the crime was usually the market place or bazaar near-by, where quarrels were frequent and weapons such as knives, daggers and revolvers were constantly employed. Murderous assaults and hand-to-hand fights were repeated almost daily, and the police seldom took notice of the disturbance. Men were often pointed out in the open road who had half a dozen or more murders to their credit. Mr. Hawes saw one hovering near his hut who had slain eight victims, and it seemed inexplicable that such a miscreant should be suffered to be still at liberty. His immunity was due to his prompt escape into the *taiga* or wild, wooded interior. Convicts who did so might be captured some day, but were seldom identified or there was insufficient evidence to secure their conviction. The authorities, too, were generally callous when one villain murdered another, philosophically saying, "After all the brutal crowd has been well diminished by one." Of course if an official was murdered, more serious steps were taken to bring the offender to justice. A Saghalien murderer was known to have committed the capital offence nineteen times, and still evaded punishment.

Female murderers were plentiful enough on Saghalien, and one of the most remarkable was a certain Sophie Bluffstein, commonly called the "Golden Hand." As a criminal, she had few equals among wrong-doers in any land. She was a Jewess, who, as a girl of rare beauty, had married a man of her own race, a financial agent, but she left him when his affairs became entangled. She developed into a cosmopolitan adventuress who made the capitals of Europe her stage, and was well known in London, Paris, Vienna and St. Petersburg. Her business was to victimise tradesmen and attract lovers over whom she gained extraordinary influence. Her frauds were extensive and on the well-known lines. She lived in great style in a smart house, in the most fashionable part of the city, and drove in her carriage to the best shops where she made large purchases of jewelry and valuables, for which, of course, she never paid. Her depredations were on a colossal scale and she was "wanted" by the entire police of Europe.

Sophie Bluffstein's personal fascination was unrivalled. Her chief charms were her wonderful eyes, which seemed to have had magnetic effect upon her admirers and drew them irresistibly to her feet, tempting them to commit any crime to secure her good graces. One of her greatest triumphs was the beguilement of the governor of Smolensk, where she had been arrested and incarcerated. Her influence over him was such that she induced him to connive at her escape, to desert his wife and family, and to accompany her in her flight. The connection was brief, and she resumed her evil courses, until she was caught in a trap at a gay supper party of young men, some of whom were terrorists, and which was broken up by the police. Arrested as a political offender, she was sent to Siberia, where in due course she escaped, was recaptured and deported to Saghalien.

Here she renewed her criminal activity, and when released from prison to enter the free command, she gathered round her a choice collection of the worst characters, whom she employed as her tools in the crimes she planned and had carried out. In one case, a merchant, carrying on his person a large sum in rubles, was robbed and murdered. The money was so cleverly buried by her that it has not yet been discovered. Her operations were greatly aided by a ship her confederates had seized and openly used as a pirate craft. To check her villainies, she was shut up at last in the testing prison at Alexandrovsk and kept constantly handcuffed. Yet she eventually regained her liberty, and after living more peaceably for a time at Rikovsk, she was allowed to settle at Vladivostok, where she kept an inn until her death.

That life was held cheap at Saghalien will be shown by the following story. A merchant of Alexandrovsk had reason to suspect his wife, a young and beautiful Tartar woman, of infidelity, and when he upbraided her she ran off and left him. She was never seen again, and it came out afterward that he had hired an assassin at the price of twenty-five rubles to kill her, according to the provisions of the Mahometan law. The assassin and his employer quarreled over the ghastly business, and the latter simplified the matter by hiring a second assassin to murder the first. But the second murder was not so successfully accomplished as the first; the victim escaped; the merchant was arrested, and a witness came forward to say she had seen him preparing a noose to hang his wife on his own account. No arrest was made for some time, and even the merchant was let out on bail.

Thefts and highway robbery were of constant occurrence, and burglaries also, both of private houses and government stores. There was a large floating population of desperadoes, which was continually recruited by the fugitives from justice, prison-breakers and vagrants from the free commands, and exile settlers who preferred depredation to industry. The *brodyaga* was a greater scourge in Saghalien than in Siberia, another and a potential check to the development of the colony on account of the terrorism exercised over the well-disposed settler, whom he robbed and maltreated. They worked generally in organised gangs, armed with stolen rifles which they readily used. The most dangerous gang was that of which the chief and captain was the notorious Barratasvili, the Robin Hood of the island, whose feats are still remembered.

Barratasvili came to Saghalien first as an exiled forger, and he passed through his prison probation with an exemplary character. He was looked upon as a mild and well-disposed man, quite amenable to discipline. When he joined the free command, he became a domestic servant and continued to be well-conducted until suddenly he ran off and escaped to Nicholaevsk on the mainland. He was pursued, taken and brought back to Saghalien, only to give his escort the slip and gain the recess of the forest, where he all but died of starvation. By the murder of a merchant on his way from Dui to Alexandrovsk carrying the price of a horse he had lately sold, Barratasvili obtained funds and became the leader of the band which soon began to ravage the district. He was like the typical brigand, waging war with the rich but in sympathy with the poor, whom he succoured instead of attacking. He was daring and unscrupulous in his robberies, shooting "at sight" all who offered the slightest resistance. As he became more and more reckless and his crimes multiplied, the hue and cry was raised against him, and wide plans were laid to capture him, all of which he successfully evaded, still boldly showing himself where he was most "wanted."

On one occasion at Alexandrovsk, a strong detachment of soldiers searched the town, house by house, in the small hours of the morning, bent upon taking him, but quite fruitlessly. Yet four hours after the search had begun, he was seen by a friend in the neighbourhood passing along the street with no more disguise than being muffled up in a fur-lined coat. Again, he entered a store in the town and having posted a sentry to keep watch, proceeded to ransack the place, emptying the counter cases of their jewelry, the tills and the safes of their cash. The recklessness of these thieves was so great that they entered the town and had their photographs taken.

But the net was closing round Barratasvili. A combined effort was set on foot to put an end to him and his gang. It was winter time when the end came. Overcome with fatigue, he one day ventured off the road into the forest close to a deserted saw-mill, and with his companions fell asleep. An overseer, trudging along the road, noticed the tracks of his skis, and they aroused his suspicions. Ordinary travellers do not leave the road to plunge into the deep snow of the dense forest. He, too, was tired, but he went back to Derbensk and secured the assistance of a posse of soldiers. Following up the track, step by step, through the forest, they came upon the long-sought robbers resting. The alarm was given. Firing began on both sides. The leader of the gang was hit in the left shoulder, but still continued to fire. The soldiers sought shelter behind tree trunks. Barratasvili, in taking aim, exposed his head and in so doing was shot in the forehead. Their leader killed, his companions threw down their arms, were taken and beaten by the soldiers with the butt ends of their muskets. In encounters of this kind, the soldiers, furious at the loss of their comrades, treat their captives most brutally, and in some cases the latter have died from injuries thus received. Three of the four companions of Barratasvili were hanged at the corners of the testing prison at Alexandrovsk. In theory, capital punishment is supposed to have been abolished in Russia, but the sentence is still passed by court-martial and the island of Saghalien in under martial law. These *brodyagi* were really strangled, not hanged. A rope with a slip-knot was fixed round the neck of the culprit, the other end being carried up and made taut to a crosspiece supported by two upright poles. The convict stood on a box, which was kicked away from under his feet, and strangulation often tardily ensued.

The *brodyagi* had little hope of permanent evasion. Now and again a few determined fugitives have seized a boat and attempted a passage across the sea to the mainland. They might win through the dangers of the sea, having evaded the native trackers, half savage men of the Gilyak tribe, more ready to shoot down than to capture, and they might make good their landing at Cape Muraviev or Pogob. But they must face starvation and almost certain death from the terrible winter cold. The alternative is voluntary surrender, with the certainty of flogging and a prolongation of sentence. More frequently, the *brodyagi* infest the *taiga* and hang about the sparse settlements on the chance of plunder, or, if in any numbers, combine for a descent upon the villages. In one year, 1896, nine convicts who had escaped from the Alexandrovsk prisons at various times joined forces in the Timovsk district and gave a great deal of trouble. They were pursued by strong parties of soldiers, but often turned to show fight, having become possessed of firearms. Eventually they were captured, the survivors of the gang ending as usual upon the gallows.

When they are Chinese—and in Manchuria, the Russians hunt them down and shoot as many as they can at sight—those wounded and taken alive are decapitated and their heads hung by the way-side, but no real attempt has been made to rid Siberia and Saghalien of this great pest and danger.

Statistics are not helpful, as so few arrests are made, and so few crimes discovered. Garroting is the chief device of the footpad. With a short stick and a noose of twine, he approaches his victim from the rear, slips the cord over his head and strangles the man, woman or child, who is unable to utter a cry; then he strips from the body everything likely to lead to its identification, and decamps. If there is an accomplice, he blocks the stranger's advance or engages his attention at the correct moment. Nor is there perfect safety in numbers. "Whilst at Khabarovsk," says a recent traveller, "I paid a visit to one of the lone pioneers of Anglo-Saxondom in that far-off land. There, within a stone's throw of the governor-general's house, three citizens were attacked within five minutes of our passing. Their assailants got away, but all three of the merchants succumbed to their injuries. At Blagoveschensk, in broad daylight, between two and three o'clock in the afternoon, and quite close to the main hotel and high street, I heard a series of revolver shots, and turning, saw a man leisurely reloading his revolver. His victim, a woman in this case, never uttered a cry, merely fell. The street was almost deserted, and the people who heard and saw took very little notice, but with the aid of a passing soldier, we arrested that man, and in the rough and ready lock-up to which he was taken were electric lights and telephone. In a few minutes the district superintendent was summoned, but we were scarcely thanked for our part, and we were told that our action was not Siberian, and that the affair was none of ours.

"From Cheliobinsk to Vladivostok crime is equally common. In the latter place, I was told that after each pay-day at the naval fitting yard men were missing and never returned. On one occasion thirty disappeared, and ordinarily eight or ten bodies are found within a few days, stripped of every shred of clothing, their tattooed marks gashed over and the features hacked so that they could not be recognised. Russians suffer more than the Chinese, and Russians are usually the aggressors. Policemen are too few and too wary. Unless the street be crowded, men may shout loud and long before any will venture to their assistance."

The suburbs and villages in Siberia, says the same authority, suffer from the vagrant bands who raid settlements and houses, exacting all they dare and often not falling short of other crimes. They are the fugitives from justice, escaped criminals, the reckless and daring convicts who have eluded their prison guards. They have nothing but what they have stolen, a wooden staff and a short length of leather or twine. Whoever gets into their power has a short shrift and theirs is not longer if they are captured in the act or traced. For entering and robbing a church in Vladivostok, some were hanged, for in Siberia the death penalty is not in abeyance as in Russia. In Siberia—and in Russia too—lynch law is common among the peaceable, industrious, well-to-do peasants as it is also among the half Russianised natives. One method of dealing with cattle thieves is to bend down two straight young birch trees, tie the hands of the robber to one and his feet to the other, then release the trees and hurry away.

Later records describe the extraordinary career of a convict, Nagorny by name, who is said to have escaped seven times from Saghalien, his last having been effected while he was chained to a wheelbarrow. This man had been guilty of more than fifty murders and several hundred robberies, many of these having been perpetrated in the disguise of a gendarme, when he entered the houses of his victims under the pretext of making an official search. He was tall, strongly built and had a ruffianly expression. When he was arrested, Nagorny pointed a loaded revolver at his custodian, but the lock of the weapon proved damaged and it was useless.

A hideous story is preserved in Saghalien of a tragic event that occurred in the summer of 1892, when a party of a hundred convicts were sent from Alexandrovsk to make a road through the *taiga* to Rikovsk. It was a terrible task; the road followed the course of the Boroni River, in a wide and swampy valley, rendered impassable by unexpected heavy rains, which cut the workmen off from their base of supplies. Great numbers of the gang perished from starvation, dysentery and fevers. Three of them, maddened by their privations, escaped into the *taiga*, and when pursued, wandered further and further into the primeval forest. It was strongly suspected, but never proved, that one of the three was killed and eaten by his two comrades, for one of them when caught was found to be carrying a human bone in his pouch, but his mind was unhinged and he could give no coherent account of what happened. He was treated as a lunatic, and his insanity saved him from punishment, but he was ever afterward known as "Vasiliv the Cannibal." The other fugitive, Kalenik, was sentenced to ninety-nine strokes of the plet, which killed him.

Political exiles have been deported to Saghalien, but not in any great number. They were among the earliest convicts transported by sea, and it is worth noting that the Russian government in 1888 was anxious to make no distinction between them and the common criminals. Mr. Kennan prints a letter concerning some of them from M. Galkin Vrasski, the well-known chief of prison administration, directing that no difference should be made between them and the ordinary criminals. They were to be subjected to the same discipline, but to be kept under stricter surveillance, if anything, and were to be liable to more severe punishments inflicted on Saghalien and in Siberia. Two, indeed, were flogged at Alexandrovsk, after an unhappy collision with the prison authorities caused by the neglect of one of them to raise his hat on meeting a subordinate official. Their sufferings were, of course, greater owing to the remoteness of their domicile and their savage surroundings. They were naturally more in touch with the civilised world at Tobolsk, Tomsk and Irkutsk, and were at a peculiar disadvantage on Saghalien, because of the dearth of educated people among the exiled population. They were in request for more cultured employment as schoolmasters, accountants or in scientific labours. As a rule, they bore their expatriation and the hardships of their daily life with equanimity, and were quiet and well-conducted. Many of them had been victims of Russian despotism and had suffered much in the Russian state prisons. One of them whom Mr. Hawes met on Saghalien was a lady who had at one time belonged to a secret society unknown to her husband. When Alexander II was assassinated she fled the country. On returning later to Russia, she was arrested on suspicion, but her identity could not be proved until her husband was tricked into recognising her when they were suddenly brought face to face. This lady was consigned to the fortress of Schlüsselburg, and was so entirely lost sight of that her husband, presuming she was dead, married again. Ten years later he heard that she was alive and had been transported to Saghalien. Having somehow settled matters with his second wife, he followed his first to the other end of the world and was eventually allowed to settle with her at Vladivostok.

In spite of restrictions, hardships and almost intolerable conditions, the political exile has been a distinct aid and valuable factor in the settlement and development of Siberia, carrying with him ideals and standards and a degree of intelligence far in advance of the native Siberian settler and peasant. The infusion of such an element is all the more needed because of the low average of intelligence of the great mass of the convicts, many of whom become permanent residents of Siberia. Mr. Henry Norman has said of the prisoners in the prison of Irkutsk, as he found them: "Never has it been my lot, though I have visited prisons, civilised and uncivilised, in many parts of the world, to see human nature at such a low ebb.... From this point of view, Russian criminology has a task unknown in countries where civilisation has reached a higher average of development." It is the criminal exile who has been a bar to progress in Siberia, and with the cessation of the transportation of this class of convicts, the future is brighter for the great exile territory which is so rich in natural possibilities.

Siberia will no doubt become the granary of the world. Its millions of fertile acres must ere long develop its great food producing qualities. With its great stretches of prairie waiting for the plough, its huge forests and magnificent waters, "it is evident that the Siberia of convicts and prisoners is passing away and the Siberia of the reaping machine, the gold drill, the timber yard, the booming, flourishing new town is awakening into new life."

The present condition of Russia is appalling. Centuries of autocratic rule, backed by barbarous methods, such as have been set forth at some length in the foregoing pages, have culminated now in a social upheaval that threatens the collapse of a vast empire. The stability of the government is wholly undermined; long continued, merciless repression has failed; resistance to constituted authority becomes daily more daring and embittered. The Czar and his bureaucracy are more and more fiercely and systematically assailed, despite the increased reprisals of despotic power and the temporary triumph of a reactionary policy.

Rulers, with their backs to the wall, plead these outrages are imperative in self-defence. The malcontents, ever increasing in numbers and violence, have openly determined to make government impossible and that terrorism by bomb-throwing and assassination is the only argument left. They will accept no compromise; they distrust all promises, and move steadily on to social revolution. "We cannot call our souls our own," said a working man in Moscow to an English writer; "we cannot discuss affairs of our country without risk of Siberia; we are taxed down to the last kopeck; we are black-mailed by every petty official; we have no freedom of the press; if anybody in authority does us wrong, we have no redress ... we hate the bomb-throwing as much as you do. But it is the only argument left to us." This is characteristic of the spirit animating the "great mass of lethargic ignorant Muscovites" goaded at last to action and gaining hourly in strength and recklessness. Meanwhile the government maintains the struggle. Its persistent answer is to refuse reforms until order is restored, and it still finds champions and supporters, especially in the so-called "Black Hundred," a powerful reactionary organisation based upon an unofficial union of the Russian people.

An examination of any of the recent budgets for yearly expenses of this huge empire will show a most astonishing percentage appropriated to the maintenance of order,—the upkeep of the police and censorship of the press,—and will furnish to the intelligent observer a reason for present conditions, as well as a reason for admiring the fidelity of the educated members of the lower classes to their ideal of liberty.

Milton Keynes UK
Ingram Content Group UK Ltd.
UKHW010702080324
439098UK00004B/238